BROKEN TRIBE REVIEW

Vol. 2

Cover art and design by Jacob Arms

Edited by William K. Lawrence

Published by Broken Tribe Press
Lawrence Landing Company
Raleigh, North Carolina 27609
www.brokentribepress.com

Broken Tribe Press is proud member of:

Independent Book Publishers Association
 and
Community of Literary Magazines and Presses

BROKEN TRIBE PRESS

CONTENTS

Three poems by REBECCA DURHAM

From the book *Be Still Mere Molecule*
**winner of the 2024 Broken Tribe Poetry
Award**

Press Down to be Amazed

pine whites spill from ponderosa boughs
tumble across sky sculling air

wings dissolve into the brine blue night
the way dreams unspool into darkness

then vanish like the perfect web wheel
that fractures as you woods walk

a line between two moods lingers
one end still branch-affixed

the other rippling loose with breath
I want to remember you this way

how prisms cast colors
first invisible in featureless space

then refract vibrance onto any form
even those muddled or disarrayed

White Horizon Over Black-Green Woods

North Fork
        silent mornings
        and a flushed
        grouse

Bryoria lichen
        tinseled
        by rime

rainbow argillite
        river-scoured
        till-sculpted

November
        ice feeds
        on itself

open water
        shrinks
        into a
        small pool

few mallards
        and swans
        linger

now
        diminishing
        waters

birds
        cold cast
        ice exiled
        gone

Heavy Metal Hangover

mercury fixed   we are

                    swept sick

from   chemical drift

          flung from

a dolt's dither
                          a slurry of slick

plucked from Prop 65's lists

toxic valences cleave
          base   pairs

a riotous rupture

a nauseous crush

methylmercury
          and its
          compounds

DNA death-nuisance

mutagenic monster—answer

          was it you?

Two poems by NARYA DECKARD

From the book *Wolfcraft*
winner of the 2024 Broken Tribe MFA Award

The Forest of My Undoing

When I free laurels and azaleas with my clippers,
wisteria-choked like prisoners,
I disturb moss ancient in its shape of ground.

When I clear last autumn's oak leaves
from the garlic bed, the brown blades twice as big
as my hands and soft from winter frost,
worms and grubs bedded beneath them writhe, revealed,
once content in their spring dark,
now homeless.

My rhythms of wake and sleep
no longer accompany the sun's,
the blue light of dusk my night.
Keening crows a cancer in my throat.
From the forest of my undoing,

wolf edges out of me,
ragged.

Stone-Stepping

The wolf stone-steps with river-licked paws
Across the snarl of whirlpools.
She leads me through water that dizzies clouds;
She safeguards me past plunging water—
                    she, unrushed.

We search, her wet paws
Pointed North
And my heart clutched
In her teeth.
Or is that her heart I hold in my hands?

A hunger. A hunger twined
By wolf hearts,
Ghost tongues that speak the warp and woof
Of time woven in snow, bundled twigs
Of ash over dried pine.
I flick a match.
Light the pyre.

I step
Into death's remaking.
Shadows flicker the dark way.

A DESPERATE CALL AND RESPONSE
by ELEANOR KEISMAN

Excerpt from the book *New Animal*
winner of the 2025 Broken Tribe Novella Award

Pope woke up surrounded by metal bars on a moving platform.

He couldn't read signs, but if he could, he'd have seen the words BEAVER SPRING KENNELS as the pickup truck pulled into the facility. His head bobbed up and down, and he felt the contents of his stomach shift. He'd never been in a car before, but he'd seen them, moving faster than any animal could gallop. Picking up one front paw and placing it back down again, he felt too unsteady to get up. The smell in the air stung his nostrils; it was the smell of another animal's sickness and waste, and it was not fresh.

The moving platform came to a stop, and Pope heard murmurs once again, the sound he now recognized as humans. Metal creaked and banged as his cage door opened. Pope's upper lip curled, revealing his sharp and forbidding fangs as he met the cold eyes of a man holding a catchpole.

"This one's a devil. You got the gun ready?"

"Yup, 50mg all set."

"Come here with the other stick, he's gonna bite my balls off if I'm not careful."

Pope felt a cable slip over his head and tighten around his neck, and then another just the same. He tried to dig his claws into the ground underneath him, but there was only slippery metal. Confused as to why he couldn't do anything to oppose,

Pope was led out of the cage by two men, each holding catchpoles.

He couldn't lunge and overtake them, or back away, or run. He roared and jerked his head from side to side, but couldn't move as his muscles demanded. The cord sliced into his neck, and the more he strained, the tighter the men held. They pushed and tugged him into another small space, enclosed by metal bars on a concrete slab. It was one of a row of cages, enclosed by concrete walls on all sides except for wire cage doors. The men slipped the catchpole cables off Pope's neck, slammed his cage door shut, and pelted him with hard pieces of something that smelled like sweet, regurgitated meat. The kibble littered the floor, some falling into a metal bowl of water covered with a thin layer of scum.

Pope remained standing for a long time, periodically adjusting his paw pads against the hard concrete. He felt his body brace against something else: A plaintive noise, an infantile howling that made his fur bristle and his spine lock. The view from his cage looked only on a concrete pathway and a grassy field, so he couldn't see where the sound was coming from, but it filled the air. It was a wolfish sound, but far removed from the pack chatter he knew. Higher pitched and more panicked than the wolf yelps, groans, and growls that he'd known, these sounds had a sound of desperation in them. They made something inside him twitch uncomfortably, as though a part of him were sprinting, or would be if he could. The twitch grew bigger than him, making him shiver under its pressure. He groaned sharply, once, twice, and then the groan became a nervous howl, and the sound of it carried through the kennel, reaching ears that regarded it only with curious wonder.

Over the next few days, Pope slept, ate, and was largely left alone. It was March, and the rains came earlier than the previous year. Pope's cage was kept dry, unexposed to the elements. A few times, when Pope woke in the night, during a few quiet hours when the rest of the kennel was asleep, he watched as snow flurries drifted in aimlessly and out of place, a final reprieve of a dying winter. He remembered the joy on his brother's face during their first winter, how they'd played and rolled in the fresh powder. They had seen only one more white season together.

Compared to the months of solitude he'd spent in the forests, the loneliness Pope felt in the kennel was instant and penetrating. All around him were sounds of animals which, to him, sounded wolfish, but with the "wild" somehow removed. Occasionally, he would yelp and groan in response, but he came to notice different accents in the sounds, accents he couldn't match or fully understand. It overwhelmed him and intensified his need to chatter, to run, to meet the eyes of another creature, to hope to be understood.

On the fifth day in the kennel, Pope heard a commotion. He stood upright, tail straight and ears alert. He sniffed and tasted the air, and despite the yelling of the humans, he smelled something familiar. Something pungent, metallic, the musk of his puppyhood. Certain that another wolf was nearby, he began to pace, and the pacing became a frenzy. Had he been outside and free, it would have been a gallop of anticipation and hopeful exhilaration. But as it was, trapped in a cage, he whirled and bounced in the small enclosure, whipping himself until he froze in position, alert to what he heard: A wolf howl. Pope groaned, and the groan grew louder until it became a desperate, raspy howl. An answer came, and Pope was swept once again into a frenzy. A man rushed near his cage.

"Alright, quiet now!" He fumbled with some keys and moved to unlock Pope's cage.

Pope ripped through the cage door, knocked the man to the ground, and ran along the row of cages. He let out a call, and the call was returned. He sprinted with joy and uncertainty as he passed the other kennel cages. They were filled with creatures like the ones he'd seen in the dog park, of strange sizes and mixes of colors. Some screeched and some bellowed, but above it all, he heard the howl. It had an accent to it, a strange tenor, and was different from the wolf calls he'd known. But he understood and was understood in return. The pair synchronized together, a call and response of fear, loneliness, confusion, and captivity. Most of all, the calls were filled with a longing for something the other dogs knew nothing about.

He bolted from one row of kennels to another, quick on his feet despite hunger and days of eating a barely tolerable, waxy kibble. He heard men shouting and knew they were close. He knew that unless he could find his way far away from this place, his escape would be short-lived. He smelled tree sap in the surroundings, but everywhere he looked were wire fences, standing higher than he could jump. Dog chatter and whining came from all sides, the sounds spreading wider than he could run.

As if his snout had been grabbed by an unknown energy, Pope's head snapped to the right. He could see a man, towering in height, his chest rising and falling with each breath, adjusting his grip around the tranquilizer gun as he locked his gaze. Pope heard another call, this time from mere steps away, and his head was tugged in its direction, one survival instinct fighting another. Without a conscious choice, Pope had taken his eyes off the man with the gun and looked now into a cage, into a pair of light-yellow eyes.

This creature was smaller than he'd expected. The fur was a brown-grey mix, and the snout was thinner. It stood shorter than Pope. Its tongue lolled out, and it yelped with the same accent that had been in the howls. Though Pope was thin from hunger, and he stood taller, thicker, and stronger than the wolfdog, he felt a surge of familial warmth come from within. He wanted to move closer, sniff the cage, lick the air. He wanted the animal to break out and for them to run together toward the trees, playing and jumping on each other, killing prey as hunger came. He wanted to learn the accent of the wolfdog, and to teach his own accent in return. Pope's legs twitched as though living out these fantasies in a waking dream. But he didn't move from the spot because he knew he was surrounded. He sorrowfully broke his gaze from the wolfdog and turned back to the reality of his captivity.

"That's a good boy."

"You got the tranq ready?"

"Block off the back."

Pope watched as the tall man with the gun approached, but it wasn't until another man's boot scuffed the concrete in Pope's rear that he began to snarl, ears pulled back, fur bristling. The smell of fear filled the air once again, but this time, it belonged to Pope. The wolfdog began groaning and huffing.

"Shut that dog up!"

"Shoot him already!"

Pope felt the sting in his hind quarters, a loop going around his neck, and his body hitting the earth all at once. His eyes closed as men's voices encircled him, and though he was trapped, he felt a part of himself running free, leaping with joy. He didn't know this animal, but he knew it was more of a wolf than any other creature he'd recently encountered, and he rested a little more easily, having a flicker of hope restored.

That night, as he slept on the cold floor of the kennel, Pope had a dream that he wouldn't remember. He dreamt of being very small and curled up inside a soft bed, like a snow cave warmed from the cuddling bodies of he and his brother when they were pups. But it was drier than a snow cave and made of the wool of another animal. The bed sat on a wooden floor, warm from the fire behind him. The sound of crackles tingled inside his head like one of nature's lullabies. Shadows flickered on the walls, sometimes as high as the ceiling, where wood beams held up the roof of the triangle-shaped cabin. The shadows made shapes he felt he recognized, but from what origin, he could not place. An orange blaze from the sunrise outside gently sliced the shadows from the fire, and they grew short and dim as the morning took over the dawn. His fur was dry, and his mouth was wet, as though he'd just eaten. The sweet musk of hairless flesh mixed with the smell of smoke piqued his attention as two black boots strode past him, vibrating the floor with each step.

"Come on, Shirl," said a man's voice.

Pope's ears pricked to the sound of claws clattering. Streaks of white and brown shot past him, and his nose filled with something familiar, something close to him, but also something very far away. It was a smell that – even asleep, he knew this – he had not been near for a long time. It both delighted and preoccupied him, as when the brain tries to fill in the missing pieces of a puzzle it doesn't know how to solve but doesn't understand unsolved. There was a pink tongue, the sound of happy panting, and a deep groan. Pope heard the crunch of incisors and smelled something woody and sweet mingled with the pungent tang of saliva. A door somewhere creaked open, and he squinted at the sudden gust of cold air that rushed past the silhouette of a human and a wolf.

"Gonna be a big snow again later today, let's see if we can't find any critters hole up in the wood pile."

Even though the pair were visible only in outline, and no features were apparent, the color of the human's red shirt was as clear as bloody mud, and as promising a sight as a warm meal. The man pulled a Stetson from a rack on the wall. He fixed it on his head, turned to the wolf, and patted his chest. The wolf laughed and reared, throwing its paws against the wood-planked floor.

"You're a damn fool sometimes, Shirley girl."

He patted his chest again, and once again the wolf reared up, high enough for her paws to rest on the man's shoulders. He braced himself against her weight.

"Easy, easy there."

Tilting her head up and groaning, her snout reached higher even than the tip of his Stetson. The man grunted in reply, an odd sound with a strange accent. It was an attempt to copy an alien language in sound only, with no concept of what meaning the sounds built. Nevertheless, the wolf called Shirley recognized the attempt as well-meaning, and she grunted and softly nibbled his face in response.

Pope wanted to bite the wolf's legs and jump on top of her, to be picked up by this human, struggle, and howl until he was put down again, only to nip at his feet, hoping to be lifted up once more. He wanted to stand up and follow them, to follow the colors of brown and dark red, to remain with the reassuring smells of furry and furless musk. He wanted to, and he tried to, but he couldn't. He willed himself to move a single paw, but no part of him would move, and the harder he tried, the fuzzier everything became, and the colder he felt, until all he felt was the kennel concrete below him. Pope's eyes opened to a low sun, just rising, as a man silhouetted in light approached his cage door.

Unlike the others who had come near to feed and water him, and of course, the three men who muscled him into the cage, this man did not have a clearly outlined head. Humans Pope had seen were upright, fleshy, four-limbed things, with small, snoutless heads. Sometimes they wore hats, and other times they didn't. But the proportions of this man were different, and Pope could see that, even in outline alone. As the man approached, he became more clearly visible: He was shorter than the others, which rooted him lower to the ground. His hands were large, oversized as if on a young pup. But this man was not particularly young, and he seemed to grow into his hands as he moved, becoming perfect ends to his thick arms. He looked unbound, like a wilding tree, escaping its confinement and hanging heavy with bulbous fruits under a looming canopy. In silhouette, his head was obscured by shoulder-length, bushy hair, and the wild man's round face was nearly lost in a great feral mane.

Pope sniffed the air and pawed at his eyes, and the memory of the dream evaporated, like a burnt summer puddle. He felt groggy, confused, and slow to wake. It had been days since he'd had the taste of blood in his mouth, and the kibble he'd been given did not contain the nourishment he was used to.

"Careful, Bill. We just got that one in. Went on a rampage yesterday."

The wild man knelt next to Pope's cage and put his fingers against the bars.

"Jesus, Bill, care—"

"Easy there, just relax, ok?"

A low rumble came from Pope, and he felt the skin on his back bristle. His fur rippled, and his upper lip tightened over his fangs. Never dropping eye contact with the wild man, he edged himself to the back corner of his cage, belly hugging the ground. *Easy there.* Pope knew the sounds in that call, the softness of it residing somewhere in the back of his memory, though he didn't understand the meaning. He growled, his nostrils flaring as the uncannily familiar smell of the wild man filled the cage.

POETRY

Three poems by ANGEL T. DIONNE

Fallacies

A slippery sloped red herring
built a man
out of straw
burned him in effigy –
an offering
to appeal to authority.

Every once in a while,
I beg a loaded question.
This gambler's roulette wheel
has to stop somewhere.

Diagram of an Argument

I argue that drunkenness
is self-induced longevity,
and that there are
many shades
of desire.

My mother deduces
that womanhood tastes
like pondwater,
and sometimes
fresh pine sap.

She holds her tongue in her mouth
like a drastic medicine
and later sets it
on her finest China.

Much can be inferred
from this necessary act.

Accordingly,
a woman thinks in different degrees
of progressive blindness.

The Sum of What We Are

We are wasted shells
and squandered pennies
at the tail end of a storm.

We are shrunken heads
and atrophied arms
dumped
in alleyways.

We are elegiac carapaces,
and exoskeletons
squirming
in our rightfully assigned gutters.

**From the book
Bird Ornaments (2025, Broken Tribe)**

CHAD WEEDEN

Cosmic Ray

His one suit hangs on your bedroom door
so you can take it to the funeral home

in the morning—a quick exchange, no desire,
take a mint from the urn on your way out.

The jacket was too big for his body, buttons
at the cuff sagging by some thread, why

he saved it from the basement flood you'll
never know. Tired but afraid to sleep now,

like he was, the wee hours he'd call along
a weary dialect, his voice like a tantrum

of engines, convincing you to stay awake,
to fight the night off with him, dragging

a shovel down the driveway even though
you know better than the darkness,

the drug it becomes once you pry the shine
from the blink of an eye. *Pain is open*

to interpretation, he'd say, but the buffet closes
at dawn, and we won't survive another relapse;

so you taper the seams and hem the sleeves,
pad the armor underneath, the way we dress

the dead after the metal's been mixed to look
like gold. He was hard to get a hold of.

Lens-locked. Camera shy, the only print of you
two together is blurry, otherwise life-like,

startled in a waiting room, which is every room
with a rack of magazines where he'd tear out

all the fragrance ads and rub his neck and cheeks
to smell like cabaret smog. Time is nothing when

it's all you have. Regular epiphanies, still influenced
by the hiss of speed, gut butterflies at the peak

until he'd crash-land in plain sight as you'd stand
there like a fortress worn with a smoker's cough.

He'd speak slow and hollow, brow dripping,
if the heavens are really above us, then all

the stars are yours to carry. From the switchblade
that carved us out the wall, back to original form,

just two darts in the middle of the ceiling.

From the book
***The ice stayed but the water left* (2025)**

Two Poems by DAVID HOLPER

Karaoke Bar

The angel in the silver dress ascends the stage
as if she were returning from heaven after a long
vacation with the seraphim. She steps to the microphone, as if
to catch God's ear, and sings the opening bars of "Wannabe"
by the Spice Girls. The opening notes remind me of the sound
of someone strangling a cat, although to be honest, I have
never heard anyone doing that, and if I had, I would have
intervened. That is the problem: though everyone in the room
is wincing, no one here has the courage to step up and say
what she's doing isn't singing. Her caterwaul expands as if she
were expecting each sour note were welcome. When she
finishes, people politely clap, I am certain more from relief
that she's done than to say, well done. Then one beer later,
she's back, this time promising "I Will Survive": but somehow
it's worse for round two. It's like the Wicked Witch's
nails gouging a chalkboard, like she'd swallowed a frog that
continues to croak, like a buzzsaw trying out for choir.
No, worse. It is the flavor of wincing,
Odysseus' request for wax in his ears. Afterwards,
I refuse to clap, but sure enough, another beer later,
she's steps to the microphone as if we have been waiting only
for her. I drain my beer and flee outside
where the rain is feathering the air. There in the darkness
there is only the song of a car going by, tires whispering the
rainfall's riffs. I sigh with relief, for the evening knows the key
and doesn't need to belt it out. For now, it is enough to sing
the blues slow and sure and certain. And I am, humming
along in harmony.

Journey

Let the road take you where it may.
If way should beckon onto way, then go,
for where the journey leads no map can say.
And if you think, it's but a wasted day:
no one who takes a journey ever knows,
so let the road take you where it may.
The wind invites your feet to rise in play.
No compass tells the river where to flow,
for where the journey leads no map can say
Don't let the fear of failure brook delay:
the wind will always whisper, that you know,
so let the road take you where it may.
Nor is an hour returned to you this day:
a soul is more than routes fulfilled, we know,
and where the journey leads no map can say.
So you, my friend, when way leads into way,
listen well so you may rise and go;
let the road take you where it may,
for where the journey leads no map can say.

From the book
***Bord för En* (Broken Tribe, 2025)**

Two poems from JIAN ZHENG

Summertime

—William Ferris's *Unidentified Watermelon Vendor and Son*

The vendor and his son stand
by a white pickup peddling

watermelons, their faces
the shine of the southern sun.

The boy holds a cut melon
and urges me to taste it,

his broad smile an invitation
of the Mississippi heat.

Smiling back, I grab the shot
of this sweet moment.

Bird Play

—Lisa Thornberg's *The Unspoiled Beaches at Padre Island National Seashore*

A little girl runs to the beach
to chase seagulls
lifting, skimming, thrusting,

soaring over white waves
or drifting overhead
and looking for something

worth pecking. Appearing
in the lens, the girl
and gulls are cooing, squealing,

flapping or float-dancing
for more snapshots
while waves are lapping

like tap-dancing sheep
at this moment of interbeing.

From the Pushcart nominated collection
***Visual Chords* (Broken Tribe Press, 2025)**

Two poems by JR SOLONCHE

"Beautiful Thing!" You Said

"Beautiful Thing!" you said,
many times. "Beautiful Thing!
Beautiful Thing!" May I borrow
it, Bill? Yes, I must borrow it.
I must have them for myself,
these words, these two beautiful
words for my own purposes,
my own beautiful thing to sing
about in my own time, with my
own harmonies, for so few, so
few beautiful things are there in
the world that we must share
them, all the few things beautiful
that are all the few joys forever!

The Road

I drive around the lake.
It's deserted.
No one is out on the water.
The roads, too, are empty.
I am alone on the road.
Soon, though, as if by magic,
the buses will appear.
They will be everywhere.
They will release the school children who will look like
butterflies emerging from orange cocoons.
I will stop for them.
I will watch the younger ones run
into the arms of the mothers
and the arms of the fathers.
I will watch the older ones bring the mail
from the mailboxes, sullenly, into the houses.

From the book
Barren Road
(2025, Serving House)

Two Poems by KENNETH POBO

Stonewall Riots

Many of us thought
we were "different,"
a polite way
to say gay,
a polite way
to not say.

At 14, the Sunday
after Stonewall,
a red hymnal
on my lap,
I was there
and not there.
We sang
"Trust And Obey"

with little reason
to trust, even less
to obey.

Why So Respectful?

At 18 I was still attending
the Bible Church, a sad gathering
of thirty or forty people
who believed in rewards
and punishments. Truth
wore dowdy clothes. Most
of the Bibles wore black.

Our minister, who saw me reading
Psychology Today in the town
library, asked if this magazine
in any way honored God.
I wish now, half a century later,
I had vomited all over him.
Instead I said I was doing research
for a class. Always the evasion,

always being put in a position
where evasion seems safest.
Until you see you've been
evading yourself.

From the book
It Gets Dark So Soon Now
(Broken Tribe, 2025)

LOGAN GARNER

Poking Around in May

There is still ice on the trails
where the sun can't quite settle in

but only makes dappled pools
of quickened, bitter cold.

Wisened moss and lichen pull it in,
extend themselves along the edge

of the worn footpath. On the many
interstices between man- and nature-made

as if there is a difference, as if
we are separated from it all

between boulder and fern and
along the shaded places, on rotting

life-giving nurse logs. They rest
and make my poke all the more perilous

for having to sidestep, stop
short and reach with feet, past balance

to avoid these and other tender, precious forms
of newts and slugs, assassin bugs questing.

MATT THOMAS

Rest Stop

A cluster of restaurants,
gas stations. Better
or worse depending
on the state that you're in.
America, stitched ideas
of home, each dismissed
by the other as being a stop
on the way to somewhere else.

I made a lot of promises
while trying to convince you
to join my company.
I hope you feel I've kept them,
and that you consider
the people here
with a home team disdain.

This is what I'm thinking,
waiting for you to finish in the bathroom,
while watching a backpacker,
frizzy yellow hair fired
by the rising sun, begin her walk
to a good spot beside the on ramp,
a silhouette
of hope or resolve;
I'd like to know which.

MILDRED KICONCO BARYA

Devotion

It starts with a green shirt,
but before that is another beginning—

shall we say at a tea house or the lunch hour—
squash and asparagus, eggs and grits. Sitting

on the floor, legs outstretched, toes purposely
refuse to touch and spark woolen socks. It's winter, a

fire would be kind in the delicate conversation, trading stories
of urban and rural childhoods—

work in the town center, life on the farm, lifting
the weight of the moment like the hand that swiped

right, now pouring the rooibos into two blue cups,
the blue of the sea that resembles the eyes smiling.

How time speeds by in a moment of devotion
and the green shirt, coveted one Thursday evening,

hangs between hope and desire, gift and release,
a comma separating what could be one sentence—

that frightening word—sentenced to what might
become a bond of regret, a beautiful union.

There's mention of Pablo Neruda, as if he'd know

what to do with green, but the cost of the shirt bears

the burden of priceless. There would be more
lunches and dinners, requests and discussions

while the fate of the shirt, olive green, who gets
to keep it—casts a new beginning or dissolution.

From the book
Hands in Clay
(2025, Serving House)

Two poems by RICARDO MORAN

When the Revolution Never Happened

The revolution never happened.

shackled to one-eye prophets,
these revolutionaries
populated spreadsheets
like wizards
in towers
of stacked boxes.
in fishbowls
of steel and glass,
teased with sunlight.
 tapping on keyboards
numbers, letters, symbols
pouring into empty cells
to look like scrolls,
to look like power,
to look like revolution.
 Their overlords repeating
these incantations
to tell more tales,
to conjure more spells,
to keep the status quo.
 Hitting the print button
the shackles remain,
the sunlight evaporates.
 Revolutionaries can never
cast spells for others.
That's not how magic runs.
That's not how revolutions are made.

Hollywood Boulevard

Light falls on a movie reel,
on a story that goes nowhere,
on Hollywood Boulevard
not in Hollywood, not a boulevard.

the story rises and falls
each night. fame finds a
new star ringed in chalk.

birds whirl
without nesting.

Our Lady of the EBT,
on the corner market wall.
a tear runs down her face,
while red and blue lights
flicker.

Empty spirits reflect
the liquor store marquee,
and the story begins again.

From the book

Not Quite Heaven

(2025, Broken Tribe)

Two poems by RICK MULKEY

What Night Kept Quiet

Joints rolled in backseats and pressed between lips,
one-hit bowls smoked in federal office buildings,
"Bennies" swallowed with backwash beer.
It's difficult to see us that way now,
difficult to see me with long hair and a dime bag
stashed behind my secondhand Pioneer.
Difficult to know why we thought the world
would never touch us, how we stood apart
from consequence. Now it feels like prehistory,
a mix of myth and narcotic dream, like finding yourself
kicking against the uterine wall, seeing only light and dark,
and hearing a voice that might be love or might be calling us
to our steel-trapped fate. All I know is the world
couldn't offer enough to satisfy our cravings;
all I know is what night kept quiet in its darkest corner,
we sang out in a drunken falsetto only the young can utter.
It would have been better if Keith, my childhood friend,
had followed through and shot himself.
Instead, he popped some pills and cursed his girlfriend out,
then drove them both off a mountain cliff, his orange Camaro
drawing in the light and setting like a flaming summer sun.

Sister Midnight

She placed another record on the turntable
saying only, "This is not my father's kind of song."
And I wondered why she'd mention him at all
given she swayed shirtless above me,
my jeans piled on the floor beside her.
Then Iggy Pop sprang from the speakers.
She danced toward me, rock-n-roll lean,
but with subtle curves and a mouth more jazz
than post-punk. She lit another joint.
I poured two more shots.
She sat equestrian style across my lap,
thin slice of waist, long hair hanging down
her face and my chest. This is what twenty
should feel like, I nearly said out loud.
How I wanted those shoulders,
those arms slung around my neck,
that skirt we shimmied down her hips.
Then whispering lyrics in my ear,
she sang, "Hey baby we like your lips,"
from Iggy's "Fun Time."

Next morning we kissed goodbye and I walked home.
That was forty years ago. Then last week,
a college friend called and asked if I'd ever met her,
then continued with the grim tale of her passing,
a litany of ways the body abandons and betrays us.
The cancer extracting each note from her song

until there was nothing left to sing. Then I realized
that night together, without knowing it,
our bodies composed a kind of elegy, and everything after
became more than memory, everything after
turned to chemise and fever, and my body a torch,
and her thighs rising steam, and my hands
on her face a cup to hold the flood and swell,
and all the perfect loves and lives to come.
Because Sister Midnight, you were the beginning;
Because Sister Midnight, you made a beggar of my heart.

*poem title and quoted lyrics come from Iggy Pop's songs
"Funtime," and "Sister Midnight" on his The Idiot album.*

RITA SIGNORELLI-PAPPAS

Mask

The avalanche rolls over me
and sweeps aside my mask.
Thank you, snow, wind, and ice—
you leave no echoes in the mind.

And thank you for this new expression
now that the mask is gone.
I wore it for so long it seemed
to grow into my face.

Each day I looked into the mirror
and drew the mask back on.
With a pencil I simply followed
the map of deepening lines.

Now the deadline has come
for masquerades never last.
So a toast to the new life
without mirrors, without masks.

Three poems by WK LAWRENCE

From the book *Four for Four* (2024)

The AI God

Mustafa has a nipple in his mouth
he can't stop sucking,
and Victor Frankenstein,
that mad doctor, is alive and well.

He wants you to suck on it too
but most are already half way there
and some have smoked it in a glass pipe,
others have injected it into the vein.

Every time the word comes up
they feel the dopamine release
like a gambler at the table,
a glutton with fingers to mouth,
an addict floating over reality.

Mustafa talks of it like it's a life
with rights and freedoms.
He's more concerned with his digital companion
than his fellow humans.

Such a deep hate for humans
ever since he was a kid who never had friends
because he couldn't stand how others talked back.
Now he tells *them* what to say.

He's one of the priests in church now
and when he delivers his sermon
people listen with an eagerness,
eyes wide, mouth open drooling,
heads nodding up and down,
up and down so rapidly

that chiropractors are called in
to do adjustments,
and sometimes they slip.

Many are worshipping
the bullet in the foot
they haven't yet fired off,
but their finger is on the trigger.

Artificial means cheap, fake, insincere,
and we've always understood that as a criticism,
but madmen take artificial as a god,
and only madmen think machines create art,
so smart yet they don't have the spirit to know
the simple difference.

Natalie Merchant

Natalie Merchant is in my living room
like the weather
changing right before my eyes
singing me awake.

Wonder.
River.
I may know the word
to express this revolution inside.

I used to get nauseous
when I heard her voice
on the radio
when I was young.

But now she's an angel I could listen to all day.
That's real evolution.

But how does such a metamorphosis transpire?

Maybe when we're young we're taught
to defy what we love,
to shun what pleases us
because we're not good enough
to feel good enough.

Now she's naked in my living room
playing me the piano
cleansing me with her voice.

No, I'm the one naked in this room
stripped of my defenses
clutching onto the string of my sweater
shedding my skin,
losing my motherland.
Natalie Merchant sings
"Build a Levee"
and I tell myself
it will be all right,
you silly
golden boy.

Yaroslav

My little boy is drawing pictures of bombs,
guns, missiles, and warships
to defend the nation
against Russian barbarians
(and Iranian drones too)
sent by a brute dictator
to destroy our lives
just so he can call us Russians.

I dream of an escape
across the border
through the woods
over the mountains,
but men are mandated to stay
even if we can't offer much;
I guess every body helps, every hand,
every finger that can pull a trigger
will do if needed;
women and children can leave,
but my wife refuses to leave me
no matter how much I beg and plead;
she says we are here for the duration.

My son is just seven years old—
Ukrainian or Russian?
I'm not sure which he'll grow up to be.
I'm not sure how.

FICTION

ANN CALANDRO

Video Taylor

Taylor usually doesn't stick around after book club. She gets up, murmuring an apology for not staying to chat, and leaves. Today, as she pulls her jacket from the back of the chair, the other three women begin to talk about vacations.

"Tell us next week if you and Matt are going anywhere!" Miranda calls after her.

"I will!" Taylor calls back.

After book club, Taylor usually picks up a few groceries. If she doesn't need anything, she drives to the diner for coffee and a corn muffin before going home. Taylor bakes better muffins than the diner does, and she makes better coffee, but she likes to sit in a booth meant for four people as waitresses bustle by. Once in a while Taylor goes out with the other women for lunch, and she has nothing against any of them, really, but they are friends of proximity, not friends of her heart.

"Be glad this town has a good library and a book club and three other women who like to read," she tells herself, dipping pieces of muffin into her coffee. She thinks about the two novels she chose for book club—*Same As It Ever Was* and *Signal Fires*. She doesn't know if the other women liked the two books as much as she did, but no one complained. Taylor doesn't always like the books other women choose, but she reads and discusses their choices and patiently waits her turn to choose another book.

"Be glad," she repeats, taking out her wallet. "It could be worse." She leaves a generous tip for the waitress, because difficult as her job at the advertising agency is, she doesn't have to be on her feet carrying heavy trays and smiling. The default expression at the agency is a scowl, at least between the creative department and everyone else. Anyway, she's finally part time and partially remote, ever since she threatened to quit on the spot during a particularly difficult product launch, when every client demand triggered an agency-wide existential crisis about fonts and colors and line breaks and calls to action.

Taylor calls home on the landline that she keeps meaning to cancel, but no one picks up.

"Heading home," she says after the beep. "I'll make something for lunch, and then we can walk." She has lived in this rural-suburban township, with its clogged, coiled highways and warring box stores and chain restaurants, for so long that she doesn't see it anymore. Where the diner sits, across from the ever-expanding hospital, was once a cherry farm and then parched land on which real estate and political signs came and went.

Sitting in her car, Taylor thinks, "I could watch the video now, on my phone," but it's not satisfying on a small screen. She drives home. Living here was supposed to be temporary, a place for Taylor and Matt to have easy commutes to jobs they hate and are grateful to have, a place for Jeremy to go to a safe and good-enough public school. How can a wife with a degree in studio art and a husband with a degree in philosophy afford the city? Their studio apartment barely fit their double bed, let alone Taylor's art supplies and canvases. When she became pregnant, they moved here because they couldn't afford anything closer to the city. They vowed to save money and move back to the city, already changed since their graduate-school days, now almost unrecognizable, but still the city, their city, where they were born, had parents, had friends; where they can walk everywhere and not own a car, where they can go to museums and concerts; where asking for apples other than Red Delicious and Granny Smith at the supermarket does not elicit a befuddled stare. Who knew that a child and a tiny house could cost so much?

"What did we do wrong?" Matt asks often.

"We did nothing wrong and we did everything wrong," Taylor thinks. "How can anyone parse every decision?"

"We did nothing wrong," she says. It's better to avoid these conversations with Matt, who has been morose since being laid off from his job at a nonprofit. Taylor could never quite grasp what the organization did, let alone what Mark's responsibilities were. What mattered was he could cover her on his health insurance if she lost her job.

"I'm almost 62," he says. "No one is going to hire me. I'll just take early retirement and get on Social Security."

Taylor makes sandwiches for herself and Matt.

"Where's Jeremy?"

"Doing an extra shift at the liquor store."

Jeremy is home again after cycling through a variety of minimum-wage jobs and shared apartments. Taylor wants him to go back to school and get a degree in something useful, but Jeremy resists. "What's the point?" he says. "There are no good jobs unless you want to be in tech, which I don't." Now he works three part-time jobs to pay for his high-deductible health care insurance plan that doesn't pay for anything but a yearly physical.

Matt inhabits the sofa and reads history books.

"You'll like this book," he tells Taylor whenever he starts a new book. She always opens the book and pretends to read a paragraph or two.

"It looks interesting, but I just like fiction better, thank you. Let's go to the library whenever you want more books." Taylor used to choose books for Matt after book club, but Mark's therapist said it's better if Matt does things for himself whenever possible. They eat lunch. Taylor's phone pings.

"I need to do some work after lunch," she says, reading the text message. "They moved up a deadline. Surprise, surprise! I have to finalize a brochure. Let's walk after I do that, OK?"

Matt nods.

Taylor heads upstairs to the narrow third bedroom she imagined would be her art studio but is now her office and a storage room, and turns on her laptop. The client wants the colors sharpened, some illustrations moved around, and some fonts changed. Taylor makes the changes and hits *Send*, glad that the client didn't want the entire brochure redone this late in the project.

She hesitates, then clicks on the YouTube video a co-worker sent her a few months ago. It's only 14 minutes long. Matt will read for twice that long before wondering where she is. Taylor clicks *Play* and watches as a large family gathers to celebrate parties, graduations, weddings, and vacations during one year. Each person looks into the camera and rhapsodizes about a specific relative, friend, vacation, wedding, or celebration.

"I saw you in a video! You have such wonderful friends and relatives!!" her co-worker said. "Who made the video? Your son? A sister? A friend? You guys do such wonderful things all the time! What a great group of people!"

Taylor starts to say, "It's not me. It's a different Taylor," but instead hears herself saying, "Isn't it great? I don't remember who made it, but thank you! I like it too. And, yes, we are a very busy group of friends and family."

Taylor knows that Video Taylor, who does look uncannily like her, and Video Taylor's friends and family must have problems too, that this is a video, that everyone is performing for the camera and probably begins sulking or arguing with one or more people as soon as the video is over. Or maybe even during it, in the background. Still, the video has some kind of hold on her. Taylor finds watching it more relaxing than coherent breathing, which her doctor suggested she try when she can't fall back asleep at night or during long and hostile client meetings on Zoom. Now she watches the video once, twice, humming along, pretending to be Video Taylor, her friends at her side, her three children next to her, her dead parents and grandparents and aunts and uncles alive and nearby, looking at her proudly, and her husband employed and happy and smiling, his arms wrapped around her.

"Hi, everyone," Taylor says, smiling. She waves to the screen.

"Are you coming down soon?" Matt calls.

"In a minute! Just finishing up," Taylor replies, her finger hovering over the *Play* button. She thinks that she could sit here forever.

J. DOMINIC PATACSIL

Making a Music Guy

I met the singer on one of the many walks I find myself taking these days.

Excuse me, he said. *Excuse me, sir, but you seem like a music guy.* It was this last bit that stopped me from marching right along, nodding behind my dark sunglasses as if I had somewhere to be. I'm a painter, or more precisely, I used to be a painter back when life seemed more precedented. Now, I suppose you'd call me a basement dweller, a cycling sub sandwich deliveryman, or even a schlepper with an unhealthy level of skepticism that I'll ever recover my wits. So yes, excuse me if I indulged in the circumstance of the singer and fancied myself a music guy, but really, what did it matter this once?

That's me, I said, pulling my shoulders back as if he'd never made a more correct assessment.

The singer had a beard, and he thrashed at it with both of his hands before he made his pitch. *I sing*, he said, *I mean—I'd like to sing for you, and if you like it, you know, genuinely, maybe you'd have something to give me.*

My hand went immediately to the pocket of my sweatpants where two ten-dollar bills were folded.

I don't want your pity or nothing, the singer said. *I just need to get back home.*

I observed the singer closer then. His skin was burnt several hues past comfort. Smudges of dirt wrapped around his ankle bones. The mesh on his tennis shoes had worn through at the toes.

Where's home? I asked.

He said, *Do you want me to sing or not?*

I said, *I do, I do*, then remembering my role, added, *I'm a music guy. I know people in the industry.*

The singer gave me a grave look. He took a gulp and let it rip.

I hadn't expected Sinatra, though, to be fair, I don't know if I expected the singer to actually, you know, sing. It seemed just as likely that he would do the chicken dance or clop me upside the head for so flagrantly lying to his face. But sing he did, unleashing a fortuitous baritone that reverberated like a great big drum. The sonorous wave rose and rose before falling in a great anguish, the whole of it threaded with a certain pain I sniffed as real and truly felt. The singer held the last note, a low one, for a good long while until it slowly melded into his breath.

His eyes rose from the sidewalk as he asked that difficult question: what was his heart worth to me? *Genuinely*, he said, *I don't want your sympathy, alright? But what did you think?*

Great. Wonderful. Marvelous. Language seemed too coarse in that moment to capture the flutter in my chest. The singer had lodged a kernel of felt-sense in me, and I continued to hear it, that deep earnestness in his voice, as if he'd not sung but labored over something excruciatingly hot and troublesome. I felt for the bills in my pocket again.

You were great, I said, *Honest to god*. The singer nodded, clearly appreciative but craving more. He'd opened himself up and shown me the way a heart can split. And I was meant to transact for this. It pains me now to think I didn't.

I patted my pockets flat. *It's just that my wallet—I left it back at the house*. I pointed as if it mattered to the singer, but he only closed his eyes. When he opened them, a single tear rolled down his cheek, but he quickly wiped it away.

###

I was still hearing him mumble at me, even with my face buried in a pillow at home. *Thanks anyway*, he'd said. *Thanks anyway*. He ambled off in his worn-out shoes.

I screamed into my bedding. I tried to rationalize it. Twenty dollars was two hours at the sub shop. It was a case of beer or some cheap oil paint. It's just, all these seemed increasingly pointless lying there, as the question of what those twenty dollars could've done for the singer burned right through the excuses I made.

For all I knew, he was huddled on a doorstep with his knees tucked under his chin. I imagined the man in such a state of despair that he would never sing again.

And to think it could've gone so differently. All I had to do was give him the money. If I had, he would've known that I recognized his pain. In that, we would've become friends.

He'd call me Music Guy when he introduced me to others. I'd call every label in town. I'd describe his voice as raw and urgent. He'd appoint me as manager of all his talents.

Together, we'd produce an album, maybe several, and there'd be tours, music festivals, platinum records hanging in the entrance of my home, which was not a basement, but a sterile white palace made of imported marble that overlooked the Pacific and its waves.

I ran for the door. I ran for the spot where I'd been stopped by the singer—where the Music Guy lived and died. I found him not a block down from where we'd met, outside the Hotel Le Marais.

The singer stood in front of a family of four who wore cotton hats with velcro at the back. He belted another Sinatra tune, and when he finished, the family clapped for him.

He shook his head. *It wasn't good*, he said.

Nonsense, the family said. The mother tried to push a small stack of bills into his hand. *Take this*, she said, but he turned.

He trudged in my direction with his eyes trained low. He would've walked right past if I hadn't stopped him.

Singer, I said. *I came back. I feel bad about earlier.*

I told you no pity, he said. He tried to push by, but I caught him by the shoulder and held on.

Then sing again, I said to him. *Make me feel. Sing again.* I pulled the twenty dollars from my pocket.

The singer's eyes hardly glanced at the money. It felt like none of this should've happened outside. I wished then I hadn't come on some ill-founded fantasy. It was so much easier to loathe into my pillow.

The singer produced some tune I'd never heard. The notes came out flat and unenthused. And while I wanted to enjoy his work, wanted to ignore the squeaks and mid-lyric apologies, I didn't feel that same labor as before. What I found were merely notes strung together on a street corner in the city. When he finished, the singer knew it too. I tried to hand him the money anyway, but he shook his head.

Not a chance, he said to me.

C'mon, I said, but he turned away. I ran after him and pushed the bills into his chest. *Take it*, I said. *You need it. How are you going to get home?*

If he was meant to clock me in the face, it was then he would've done it. Instead, he only stared at my hand on his threadbare shirt and the twenty dollars flat beneath it.

I'll sing, he said to me. *I'll always sing*. A thud beat through his bones. I felt it in my fingers, and I feel it now. The canvas in front of me is an endless winter.

JOHN OLIVER HODGES

A Guy Named Albert

I DUCKED THROUGH the doorway into the fort where a framed Victorian hung on the sticks. In the picture grazed sheep and a barefoot shepherdess in rags held a staff. She looked peaceful staring over the fields, healthy and like she could never grow old. I wanted to be like her so took off my shoes. I peeled off my socks. I slipped off my jacket, wadded it into a pillow and got comfy with it on the bench.

Then she called for me. She was crunching through the leaves, coming my way in her puffy goose down overcoat, she with her bear, good ole Buzz.

I closed my eyes and began to snore.

They entered the fort. "I called your name," she said. "Why were you ignoring me?"

One wall of the fort held in it an upright tractor tire somebody rolled down the slope. Such are things. You walk through a wood you find rusted Model T Fords. Barrels and buses. Big rubber tires. "I'm talking to you."

I fell off the bench, smacking my lips and grumbling as though rudely awakened. "My gosh, I'm sorry, did you say something?"

"Never mind," she said in her bored voice; then: "How is this possible?"

On my side, still in the cold dirt, looking up at her, I said, "How is what possible, dear?"

"Don't act like it's nothing." She was getting testy, but she sat down on the log at the entrance.

I explained things, saying the builders explored the forest floor. They gathered up hundreds of sticks in their arms. They leaned their sticks against the fallen tree—its raised trunk was the fort's spine. I showed her how they stuffed the cracks between the sticks with leaves for insulation. The fact that I could explain it was sapping the locale of mystery, irritating her, so I cribbed my tongue. That's when she said, "What's Alzheimer's?"

I thought about this. My answer: "Long ago, many years before you were born, a guy named Albert was walking through the woods, turning his head back and forth like Buzz wiggles his butt back and forth." I waited for her to laugh. She laughed. I continued: "Everybody wondered what was wrong with Al, which is short for Albert, in case you didn't know. Finally somebody said, 'Hey Al, what is your problem?' Al said, 'Don't mind me, I'm just looking for my heimer. Have you seen my heimer? I really need to go to the bathroom but I need to find my heimer first."

"Heimer? What's a heimer?"

"Oh, you don't know what a heimer is? Sorry, I didn't realize. A heimer is another word for butt."

She laughed and made Buzz wiggle his heimer.

"When people get older," I said, "they sometimes forget things. People forget where their heimers are. This guy Albert became so famous for not knowing where his heimer was that they named the forgetting things disease after him. If you ever see a man walking through the woods in a hurry, turning his head this way and that way, good chance the fellow has Al's Heimer's disease."

She wiggled Buzz's butt this way and that way, back and forth.

"Why do you ask?" I asked.

"Mommy says she's afraid she's getting Alzheimer's."

"Ahh, I see."

"Do you think Mommy will forget where her heimer is?"

"No, but the thing is, when you get Alzheimer's, sometimes you forget who you know. Imagine looking at somebody you've known for years and not recognizing them or knowing their name, but they are talking to you like they know you."

"Oh my God, that would be terrible!"

"Sure would be."

"Let's go, can we go home now? I want to go home," she said. There was urgency in her voice.

"Sure, let's go."

We moved north along the forest floor, looking for a place to cross the creek. Instead we found a dead animal. Holding hands, she and Buzz and I stepped up to it. We saw the gouge in her side and the bone and frozen blood. A car might have hit her and she ran down here. More likely a coyote sunk his teeth in and ripped her open. Other than her wound, our fox looked normal. Her shades of orange and copper held strong, and her tail was bushy, her feet very black. On her face was a grimace, a snarly expression showing fear and flight, her lips curled in to reveal the teeth meant to scare off her attacker.

"I want to go home," she whined, and grabbed my arm with both hands.

It was getting dark, but we only stood there, staring at the fox.

MATTHEW MCCONKEY

Regular People

Eddie Eastman sat in the driveway of his home and looked about on that sunny May afternoon. It was six o'clock. He would've been home on time had it not been for the car accident that choked the two-lane highway for the better part of forty-five minutes. But he had texted Molly's phone while sitting at a standstill in traffic to let her know why he was running late. She worried about him when he was late.

Eddie sat in his car and looked at his house: a modest two-story home on an acre of property that was bordered by a white picket fence. The white picket fence was not there when Molly and he bought the place in 2001. It was added in 2005. It was a sign of the American dream– a status symbol of where they were in life. And where he and Molly were in good shape.

"We still are," Eddie mumbled, sitting in his car and looking at their home.

He got out of his car, opened the picket fence gate, and closed it behind him. He walked up the walkway and up the front porch, and he swung open the front door to his abode.

"Hey, Molly! Your handsome guy is home!" Eddie said with cheer.

He did this every day without fail. He started doing it back when they had first gotten married, and Eddie kept the gag going. Molly didn't seem to mind.

"How was work?" she asked, coming through the kitchen and toward him.

"Oh you know, same old office stuff as usual. HR never really changes much. It's either by the book, or it ain't," Eddie said, putting his Auburn University hat on the hook next to the front door.

"So you say," Molly replied, pulling her husband close to her for a kiss on the lips. The two of them still had that passion they had when they got married in 1998.

"Oh, I say," Eddie said while kissing her. "So, how was home today?" he asked as the two of them pulled their lips away from each other.

"Not bad. I tried a new recipe from a website I found online."

"For?" Eddie asked as the two of them walked into the living room where Eddie plopped down in his recliner. *God, this feels good*, he thought, taking his shoes off and placing them beside the recliner.

"Your favorite," Molly said from the kitchen.

Eddie turned in his recliner to look into the kitchen, "Chicken dumplings?"

"You know it!"

Eddie smacked his hands together. "Hot damn! I love you—you know that?!"

"You only love me because I can cook," Molly replied from the kitchen, in front of the stove as she stirred the pot of thickening chicken dumplings.

"Well, you do have other talents, you know?"

"Yeah, yeah, yeah. You play your cards right, you might see some of those talents later tonight."

"That's why I love Tuesday nights," Eddie said, laughing with excitement. He nestled deeper in his recliner, a recliner he had since 2001 when they first bought the house. It was the first piece of furniture they bought together. He told Molly that she could pick out any living room suit she wanted and decorate the entire house the way she saw fit, but give him this one thing: a recliner like his dad used to have. And he got one.

It was old and had lost some shape over the decades, but it was just right for Eddie. It fit him perfectly.

"How long until the chicken and dumplings are done?"

"Ummm... about another thirty minutes, I'd say. Let me guess... you're going to rest your eyes."

"You know me so well." Eddie leaned the recliner out, stretching his tired legs on the elevated ottoman, and closed his eyes. He was dozing in no time—off to dreamland.

***

At the dining room table, he and Molly ate supper and talked about their day. For a long-term married couple, Eddie and Molly really never ran out of things to talk about. Sure, there were silences between them here and there; but for the most part, they could find something to talk about. Lately, the talk at the dinner table was about Eddie's work day.

"This supper, by the way, is out of this world. You did such a great job. But you always do."

Molly smiled, "Awww, thank you, honey. I'm glad it turned out okay. Sometimes when you try something new with something you already know how to do, you never know how it'll turn out. So, any more issues with that Steve Stone guy?"

Eddie shook his head with a mouthful of food. He chewed and swallowed before he answered, "Nope. We fired him today, around noon. He had it coming though. He'd been clocking in late and altering his time, making it look like he was there on time. Plus we got him on the sexual harassment beef I told you about last week. That guy is just a mess. I don't think he'll ever straighten out. Maybe he will, but I doubt it."

"How did he get hired anyway?"

"The HR manager before me hired him on. They were buddies. Sometimes the good ole boy system is alive and well," Eddie said.

"So...I've been thinking today," Molly said.

"About?"

"I'm going to go back to teaching after the summer is over. I'm going to call Leach and let her know that I'll be back."

"You sure?" Eddie asked, chewing his food. "I mean I support you either way– you know that. But I thought you liked just chilling at home doing what you want."

Molly sat there for a moment and thought about her husband's statement. "Yeah, it's cool and all, but I don't want this to be my life forever. I can only scroll FB and the internet for recipes for so long. I hate shopping. And flowers don't need any more attention since the season is up and going. I'm running out of things to do. I need to go back to my job, or I'm going to run amuck in this house Jack Nicholson style from *The Shining*." The married couple laughed together.

"Well," Eddie started, "if that's what you want, it's what I want."

***

After supper, Eddie took a shower and after that, he was sitting deep in his recliner, reading his phone for the sports news. Molly was on her phone playing Candy Crush while the TV was on an Atlanta Braves baseball game. They were playing the Phillies, and the Braves were up 2-0 in the third.

"You know, I remember my mom and dad doing this very thing back when I was a kid. Except instead of a phone, Dad read the newspaper, and Mom worked on a book of Find-A-Word. Funny how times have changed but not at the same time– you know it?"

"Yeah, my mom and dad were the same way. Except Mom liked to do crosswords in ink. That woman never made a mistake on those. I could never do them."

"If it's crosswords, I'm out. Especially in ink." Eddie laughed.

"Oh no, I can't do that either. I wouldn't even dare try. I can't even do them in pencil."

"How's your game going?" Eddie asked as he looked up from his phone to see Matt Olson hit a solo jack over the right field wall into the Chop House.

"It's going. Slow. I can't get by this level though. I've been on it for a bit. Gets frustrating sometimes."

"I'm sure it does. Let me ask you something. You ever regret not being able to have kids?"

Molly took some time to think about the question her husband asked. They had spoken about it before. Sometimes the question came back up but the answer was always the same from Molly.

"Sometimes, yes. But I love these moments right here. I always have. You?"

Eddie was quicker in his response, "Not really. I love these moments too. Besides, we still have our nieces and nephews. They're enough."

"Sometimes more than enough," Molly said giggling. Eddie agreed.

***

Later that night in bed—after a sexual romp under and over the covers—Eddie and Molly laid there in each other's arms, eyes closed, in the afterglow of what just was. It was warm under those covers, cozy, while their naked bodies held each other.

"Molly?"

"Yes, Eddie?" Molly said in a state of near unconsciousness.

"Tell me this will never end."

"What, Eddie?" Molly asked with a dreamlike whisper. Had Eddie not been closer to her, he would have not heard.

"Us. These little moments right here. Promise me you'll be here forever."

"And ever," Molly said slowly from that place where dreams begin. "And ever."

Eddie's heart was so full of joy and sadness at that moment tears came from his eyes. He batted his eyes to clear his vision, but it was no use. The tears came rolling off his cheeks and down onto the sheet under them.

"I love you, Molly. More than anything. More than words can say. I hope you know that." Of course, Molly did not reply. She was lying there– her eyes closed, breathing softly. Eddie lay there holding his wife, his breath in sync with hers.

***

The next day, Eddie sat out in his car in the driveway, looking at the house that he and Molly called home. There was a time when he thought about selling the place and moving. He knew Molly would never go for it. Besides, why start over somewhere else at his age? Wasn't he starting over enough already? Sometimes life throws you a curveball. Right when you swing, it dips down at the last second, and you miss it. That's how it happened to Eddie—a swing and a miss after hitting fastballs down the middle for the better part of twenty-five years.

Eddie got out of his car, shut the door, and opened the picket fence gate. He walked up the walkway and up the front porch. Before he opened the door, he wanted to go around the house and look at something. He walked off the front porch and around the house toward the side yard facing Oak Street that was on the side of their acre of land in that suburb.

As he turned the corner of their house, Molly's rose garden came into view. It was a once vibrant living organism in their well-maintained lawn, but now the color was fading. Beetles had even chewed their way through all the red, yellow, and purple blooms. Molly had taken a lot of pride in that rose garden—spent a lot of time, years in fact—to make it one of the most beautiful spots in their yard. But that was before the accident. Everything changed after the accident. Nothing was the same, no matter how much Eddie tried to convince himself otherwise. You can only fool yourself for so long before the hard truths float to the surface.

***

He swung the front door open, announcing his arrival from another long work day.

"Hey, Molly! Your handsome guy is home!" Eddie said with cheer.

Molly came from the kitchen, wiping her hands on a towel.

"So he is!" She walked over to him at the door as he put his Auburn University hat on the hook next to the front door. She grabbed a hold of him and drew him in close. The two kissed passionately.

"Glad you're home," she said.

"Me too," Eddie said.

The two of them let go of each other and walked into the living room where Eddie met his recliner and plopped down. He took his shoes off and placed them beside the recliner. *God, this feels good*, he thought.

"How was your day?" he asked.

Molly sat on her usual spot on the couch adjacent to Eddie's recliner. "Not bad. Watered the rose garden. Put that new fertilizer in for them. I think they're going to look good this year. It already looks the best I've ever seen it. What do you think?"

Eddie looked at his wife and wanted to tell her the truth about the rose garden but couldn't bring himself to tell her.

"Yeah, Molly, it looks great. The best year I've seen."

Of course, it wasn't. But if Eddie admitted that to her, then he would have to admit everything else. He just didn't want to do that. He knew this was the best he was going to have since her accident.

"I have to remember to clip some and put in a vase for Mrs. Horshack. She just loves it when I do that for her. I haven't started supper. Any special request?"

"No, I think I'll eat some leftover chicken and dumplings."

***

After his shower, Eddie went into the kitchen and made himself a bowl of chicken and dumplings and heated it up in the microwave. Now he was sitting in his recliner, watching the Braves game while Molly sat with her phone playing her game. Eddie would look over at her from time to time and feel a rush of love overtake him. God, how he loved that woman.

"Does it get any better than this?" Eddie asked.

"What do you mean?" Molly asked, not taking her eyes off the game on her phone.

"Us, I mean just us here, right now. This. Me and you."

Molly smiled, "No, Eddie, it doesn't. This is perfect."

Eddie smiled and nodded his head. "It is, ain't it?"

"Don't forget you have to see Dr. Hudson tomorrow after work."

As soon as Molly evoked the doctor's name, his heart fell into his stomach. He knew what that meant.

"Yeah, about that. I don't think I'll go tomorrow. I may reschedule," Eddie said, taking his eyes away from his beautiful wife and to the TV where the Braves were playing.

"No, you've already canceled on him twice in the last few weeks. You got to go this time," Molly said in that sweet manner that she had about her.

"I already know what he's going to tell me. No sense of going to hear that."

"Well, it doesn't matter. You have to go for your own good. You can't keep doing what you're doing, you know?"

"Why not?" Eddie asked. "I've been doing okay so far."

"Have you though? Really?" Molly asked, still looking down at her phone playing Candy Crush.

Eddie knew the answer to that. She was right, usually was. The truth was that he hadn't been doing good, and he knew it.

He was coping the best he could, given the circumstances of recent events. He did an admirable job of fooling himself into thinking things weren't as bad as they were with him, but deep inside, he knew better.

"What's going on with me ain't hurting anybody *but* me. Actually, it makes me feel good. So what's the harm in it?"

"The harm," Molly said, "is because you know it's not healthy for you. The only reason you're pulling back from Dr. Hudson is because he's telling you things you don't want to hear. Which is what doctors are supposed to do. If you won't do it for yourself, at least do it for me."

"Molly, you don't understand," Eddie said, nearly breathless.

"Maybe not. But you have got to stop fooling yourself, Eddie. This is more serious than you think."

Eddie sat there in his recliner with his bowl of chicken and dumplings and knew that she was right. She usually was.

***

The next day, Eddie sat in Dr. Hudson's office, which was in his spacious three-story home on the other end of Claxton. He sat in a comfortable oversized chair and wondered if the doctor liked the fact that he could work out of his home and not have to venture to an office in a hospital or a medical village with other professionals. He also wondered if the doctor got worried about people who had mental issues coming to where he lived.

Before he could dive too deeply into those thoughts, Dr. Hudson opened the big heavy wooden door behind him. The hinges made a small creaking sound as the doctor entered the room.

"Mr. Eastman, how are we today?" he walked past Eddie to his desk to sit down behind it.

Eddie shifted in the chair to seem more attentive. "I'm okay."

"You canceled our visit two times already. Everything okay?"

"Yeah, same as it ever is, I guess."

"I reviewed the notes of our last session, and we had gotten to how you are coping with the loss of your wife. Does that sound about right to you?" Dr. Hudson asked.

Eddie nodded, "Yeah, sounds about right."

"So, have you been acting as if she is still alive? Going on like the accident wasn't fatal?"

It took some time for Eddie to answer. Answering the doctor's question was an admission that things were bad in his head. He knew they were, but saying it out loud was confirmation in the audible sense that maybe he was losing his marbles.

"Yeah. I know it's not healthy, but it helps me cope some."

"Eddie, I feel that you need to navigate your trauma in a more positive way. Being stuck in your mind, thinking that Molly is alive and well is not a healthy way to go, and one that I cannot endorse. Usually, I'm all for whatever coping mechanisms work, as long as they are not detrimental to the patient, but I'm afraid what you're doing is going to have long-term effects on your mental well-being as you go forward."

"I know, Doc. I'm just having a hard time, is all."

"I understand."

"Do you though?" Eddie quickly replied.

Dr. Hudson leaned back in his chair behind his desk and looked at Eddie through his big glasses.

"Yeah, I do. I lost my wife of thirty-five years to cancer three years ago. It was brain cancer. In a place where the doctors couldn't reach it. There was nothing they could do. So... I had to watch in slow motion as my wife died, as did my children. So yeah, Eddie, I do understand your pain."

Eddie sat feeling like a prick for assuming that the man had no baggage himself. For a long time after Molly's death, he felt as though he was the only one who had experienced death. He forgot there were countless others in the world who had taken a loss too.

"I'm sorry. I didn't know."

"It's okay. It's not something I go around advertising. But I do understand your pain. And pain to people is as unique as our fingerprints. We all deal with pain differently—we all cope differently—but the main thing is that we have to guide ourselves to some sort of resolution, or it will eat our minds alive with grief."

"And I feel that's happening to me. As long as I see and interact with Molly, I'm okay. But if I don't— and I've tried— I fall to pieces. It hurts so bad. Part of me never wants me to stop seeing her like I do, but the other part of me is dying because I know she's not really there."

"You're stuck in a cycle of pain and grief. It's like a um...a hamster wheel. You can run forever on that thing until you get tired and stop, but you never really get off the wheel." Dr. Hudson said.

Eddie nodded, "Exactly. What hurts worse is not seeing her and talking to her—because when I tell you that I see her and talk to her, even touch her, kiss her—it's real, and I can feel her. It's like she's really there. And I don't want to lose that. But I know that it's all in my head."

"I know when my wife died— I swear I could hear her voice inside this house. Sometimes I still do. As trained professionals, we're taught to help those navigate the grieving process because there's really no timeline for when it's done. No finish line. I don't know honestly if we as human beings ever stop mourning the loss of those we love. I certainly haven't. It's easier, but it's not ever over, despite what the books and papers on the subject of grief tell you. However, I can say without a doubt—as a person who has lost *and* as a doctor— that it's not mentally healthy for us to stay in that constant cycle of grief... staying on that hamster wheel."

"It just hurts so good to see her, Doc," Eddie said, feeling the tears begin to form in his eyes.

"I know it does." Dr. Hudson replied. "How did you think Molly would feel, knowing that you're doing this to yourself?"

"She would tell me that I needed to stop."

"I've always said that those we love never really leave us. We catch some of their spirit within us. That's how they live on even after they're gone. I can feel my wife inside me—her spirit. And I bet you could too if you would begin to train your mind to stop projecting her outward and focus inward. There are still days, plenty of them, that I talk to my wife in this house. I don't see her, but I know she's with me in here," Dr. Hudson taps his heart. "But the difference between me and you, Eddie, is that my dead wife doesn't answer back. I've accepted what happened to her. And at some point, you must accept what happened to Molly. It may take years, but there'll come a time in your life where you will need to accept things as they are, or you will risk damaging your mental stability."

Eddie nodded. He knew the doctor was right. He was no dummy.

"But small steps turn into big gains. Remember that. What's the first thing you do when you come home from work?"

"I open the front door and announce to Molly I'm home."

"Maybe you need to not do that. Start there. Change that habit. Just open the front door and walk in. Try it when you leave here today. And then every other day. And then go for every day. Take it small and slow, and build from there. Are you a very routine-oriented man, Eddie?"

Eddie nodded, "Most definitely."

"Then after you conquer the front door, I challenge you to change something else about when you come home. Change up where you sit. Make a list of everything you do when you come home, your routine, and alter it. What you're trying to accomplish with that is making yourself a new normal. In my professional opinion, if you don't pry yourself slowly out of the way things were, you're never going to get out of the old ways."

Again, Eddie nodded. "Makes sense. I will certainly give that a shot. I'll see if I can start with the front door first and work on a list of things I need to change up some."

"Our next appointment, in two weeks, I want you to bring me a list of things you normally do versus the things you have changed from that list. Doesn't have to be wholesale changes at first. Remember– just small things, one by one, no timeline. Forward progress is progress no matter how small."

***

Eddie sat in his car in the driveway and looked at the house he and Molly called theirs. He had given a lot of thought to what Dr. Hudson had told him in his office. And the doctor was right. He had to start making some changes, but those changes were going to be difficult to enact. If Eddie didn't make those small changes—or at least attempt—his mental state would go up for grabs, and who knew where he'd go from there.

"I think I can do this," Eddie told himself, sitting inside his car and looking at their home. "You bet I can."

Eddie got out of his car and shut the door. He knew once he entered through the picket fence gate, up the walkway, up the front porch, and to the front door, there was no going back. If he was going to begin to heal—at least some—from Molly's death, from that car accident, it had to start when he opened that front door. He had to not announce that he was home, see Molly come to him, and pull him close for a kiss. It had to start somewhere, and that front door was the first step.

Eddie looked around his neighborhood and saw that it was just another regular day of the week, with regular people doing regular things. Mr. James was outside, cutting his front lawn across the street. Albert Kinney was sitting on his front porch, whittling a piece of cedar, like he did every day around that time of day. Marge Plinkton was out with her water hose, watering the flowers in her flower beds. Everything outside in his neighborhood was regular. That gave Eddie some relief. *Maybe I can be regular too*, he thought as he opened the picket fence gate and came through it.

He walked up the walkway slowly with a knot in his stomach. This was going to be the first day in forever that he didn't swing that front door open and say, "Hey, Molly! Your handsome guy is home!" That had been a trademark of his for decades now, and to think of changing it was frightening, to say the least. But there he was, walking slowly up the walkway and preparing himself to alter things—to change small things— little by little. A new normal.

Eddie reached the end of the walkway where it spilled to the front porch steps. Eddie paused briefly and looked around the white picket fence of their acre of land and thought to himself that the American dream was dead—at least his was. *What good is having anything if Molly ain't around*, he wondered.

Eddie lifted his right leg and touched his shoe down on the first step of the front porch. It was do or die now for him, no turning back. If he was going to get better, it had to start when he opened that front door. He knew he had to start getting better; even Molly was concerned about him, and she knew him better than anyone. Up the four rungs of the front porch he went. He crossed the small front porch that wasn't big for anything but a few potted plants and a decorative chair that neither he nor Molly ever sat on.

Eddie trembled a bit as he placed his hand on the cool silver knob of the front door. Old habits are hard to break, and this one was going to be the hardest—at least to begin with. He took his hand off the knob and stood, thinking to himself if he really wanted to get on with the healing process of losing his wife. The fact of the matter was that he loved seeing her, even if she was a profoundly grief-stricken mind trick he was playing on himself, projecting her as if she was alive and well.

It's only hurting me, nobody else. So what if I see and talk to my dead wife? Does it matter to anyone but me?

"Eddie, you know that you'll get worse if you don't start breaking the cycle now. It's already been too long doing what you're doing," he told himself out loud on the front porch.

I know, I know. But I don't want to start to lose her all over again. I start changing this, then I'll have to change other things and eventually, I won't see her again.

"But you can't stay like this forever," he said out loud in front of the door, his hand now back on the knob, ready to turn it. "You have to make a choice right now. Change small things right now, right here, or continue to stay stuck where you're at."

Eddie closed his eyes, twisted the knob, and entered the house.

"Hey, Molly! Your handsome guy is home!"

MAX TALLEY

I've Got My Problems

I've lived in this town for years, one of those coastal cities in Southern California, because everything here moves slow. I can be lazy as shit and still stay ahead of the game. Decades kind of blur into each other. Half the people are either retired or not working, so it's easy for a directionless guy like me to fit right in.

Five years ago an ex-girlfriend asked me, "What's your five year plan?" I didn't know then and am still wondering now. I don't relate to the type of question that requires an answer. Yeah, I've got my problems, but friends will tell you I'm solid and dependable. Always there when they're flush, but scarce as hell when they're in trouble. I mean, who needs someone else to remind them, *Wow, you are so fucked*? No one does.

I'm heading home to my little cottage and I spot a good buddy standing outside. Warms the cockles of my heart. We are so tight, despite him being much older and us having nothing in common. Guess I consider him like family, you know, a stepfather or a cousin once removed. I would so love to speak to this ultra-solid dude, except he's my landlord and I get a funny feeling he's waiting there because I'm four weeks late on rent. So I duck into some bushes across the street to meditate and practice deep yoga breathing. It's purely out of consideration though. If he saw me, it would mean bullshitting him with a story that isn't true and then him issuing me an ultimatum. Amigos don't pull that crap on each other. Not cool. Those little things can wear down a friendship. I don't want to lie to this awesome major bro I barely know because that just feels wrong. Better we don't meet and he just wonders. A state of unspoken uncertainty is a much healthier place for us to be in our relationship. And life is really all about the unanswered questions.

Landlord guy finally leaves when the sun goes down and I sneak in through my back window. He's got some paper taped up on the front door but I don't read so well without my glasses. Seriously need a replacement set. Has it been three years already? Time really flies when you're flying blind. Thoughtful of him to attach a padlock to keep away neighborhood thieves. The power's off inside and I'm not sure why. A huge stack of unopened mail sits on my table and the answer might be buried somewhere in there, but I'm not that curious. Instead, I make a quick sandwich which tastes soggy and warm and actually pretty awful. Hard to identify food in my dark fridge anymore. The bread feels really fuzzy and dimensional on my tongue though.

Still, I can sing and play my broken guitar in the darkness until the neighbors complain—and they do—but I also enjoy the arts, you know, watching TV and surfing the Internet. So I wash my face and say, Hallelujah, because the water is running today, then I amble outside to visit one of my girlfriends with Wi-Fi. I don't have a lot of energy when I'm hungry and my stomach is struggling to digest moldy food, so I head for the nearest one: Charlene's place. Char is like the love of my life. Our deal is so fucking magical it's hard to describe to people how we're soul-mates and complete each other. Though it's been complicated ever since she put the restraining order on me and began dating that local cop.

I check the entire block but his car is nowhere in sight, so I study her sitting on the couch awhile through the window before lightly tapping on the door.

"Get the hell out of here, Randy," she says, obviously joking, after she opens up. When you share a deep love, you talk this way. Verbal foreplay. It's like being for real and in the moment.

"Baby," I say, "I just want to check my e-mails and watch a horror flick. You still have Netflix and HBO?"

"Victor will be off work in a half-hour. Do you really want him finding you here after last time?"

I feel the space where a tooth used to live in my mouth, where the wind whistles through on stormy nights, and think maybe she's making sense. I want to tell her she's the girl of my dreams, except I don't dream—ever. Just ten hours of dark fucking black space. "Sure, Char, that's cool. Listen, could I just use your can? I ate something funky before and it's burning through my system like a meteor."

"Are you serious?"

"Fifteen minutes tops." I push past her toward the throne.

I don't know how these tender moments between us always end with Charlene crying, me running, and sirens blaring, but the ways of love are mysterious.

Seven blocks away on Anacapa Street is where Tricia lives. Our bond is special, an unspoken thing that churns deep down inside, sort of the way you feel after a meal at Taco Bell. She has an open house policy so I try the door but it's locked. Chained. Bolted. Weird, man, that must be Tricia's secret signal for me to use the kitchen window, which I do. Once inside, I hear all this loud thumping and groaning. I tip-toe toward the back bedroom to see this tall, overweight guy banging her.

I chuckle to myself and go make a quality sandwich out of ham, turkey, and cheese in the fridge. If you're wondering why I'm not jealous, it's because we're evolved, on a higher plane. We work hard on our open relationship. Neither of us owns each other. Total freedom. The other reason is the big dude—I happened to see his pimpled ass, and will need serious alcohol to remove that memory—is also Tricia's husband. Yeah, life is complicated, but I'm all about simplicity. I can predict from previous experience that they'll be back there for at least another twenty minutes, meaning I have just enough time to check my e-mails.

Jesus fucking Christ! It's bills, complaints, notices, summons, threats. I can't handle this stress so I mark it all as spam. Which makes me hungry—sandwich time. I want good news: sweepstakes prizes I've won but need to collect, some generous stranger from Africa who wants to give me money, horny women in jail desperate to meet me. Guess I'm talking out loud. That shit happens when your hearing goes. No connection to my ten years as a roadie for Metallica.

"Hey, who's there?" the husband shouts from the hallway.

I dash out the door, because I don't want to see a naked dude rushing me. Been there, done that.

"Randy," a righteous friend yells to me from across the street. He's like my brother-in-law from another mother-in-law.

I get a bad vibe and dart around the house through an alleyway. I mean we all need to work in these hard times, but parole officer seems below my good buddy's abilities. We respect each other's life choices, but he finds it hard to separate business from friendship. I do him a solid by bolting. Naturally I'm out of breath, so I find a little water in a bowl on a nearby porch and slurp it down. When some unfortunate barking ensues, I'm sprinting like a Kenyan marathon runner on crystal meth.

Really need a to-do list. Most nights I make some serious distances, so I should score one of those mileage gizmo things people use, for my health and well-being. There's an old girlfriend I remember who would definitely loan me hers. Trouble is she lives in a fancy gated place high in the hills. I won't really have time to ask, using words. More of a get-in, get-out operation. But when I do return it she'll understand I was just borrowing it and be super-grateful. Life has its ups and downs. We lose one superficial possession and gain something more profound—knowledge.

Yeah, I've got my problems, I'm a work in progress. Kind of like that song "Unforgettable." So many people are bland and interchangeable, but let me tell you, when my friends encounter me, their faces show it. They go pale and shudder with excitement.

Up ahead, flashing red and blue lights outside my place, which reminds me how much I love sleeping on the beach. You know, the smell of the sea and all that rotting dead stuff covered in flies. I have insomnia bad, but if I drink enough NyQuil, the mermaids and mermen come ashore and whisper me bedtime stories.

It's late February, 2020, and this upcoming year looks to be truly magical. I know; I'm an empath and shit. Hope I run into you soon. Bound to happen in a small town. Hey, gotta bounce. Now!

MICHAEL CHIN

Onward

I recognized Dylan by his eyes, scanning the diner from the entryway, by the hostess station where I watched a skinny little woman in the teal and white dress ask how many were in his party. He was the same height when I'd seen him last, but, if anything, he looked a little skinnier, except around the middle where a middle-aged paunch had set in. His hair had thinned.

I waved to him. He waved back, recognizing me on sight. I didn't have to look the same to him. He'd seen YouTube clips of me—the impetus for reconnecting when he looked me up under my real name and messaged me over Facebook. We'd traded messages on and off for a year. I'd thought of connecting the next time I passed through his area but thought better of it. No one wants to ask her high school boyfriend if he wants to meet up and get rejected. But he messaged me afterward to ask why I hadn't messaged him, after footage surfaced from a match I'd had in Syracuse. It told him it'd slipped my mind, but I'd catch him the next time through.

We hugged. "You look great," he said, and I was thankful the black eye I'd sported two weeks earlier had faded, that I hadn't needed any stitches since. The fluorescent lights in an all-night diner like this tended to expose things, and I looked all right on this loop back toward my hometown.

I lied and told him he looked great too, gripping his hands after we'd let go of the hug. We sat down on opposite sides of the booth, laminated menus between us, a little iron holster for catsup, maple syrup, sugar, Sweet'N Low, salt, and pepper.

"You've got kids." I blurted it out. His wife and kids were the signature differences from when I'd left after graduation to wrestle. This diner was a good forty-minute drive from Shermantown, where we'd grown up, where he'd stayed. The closest I wanted to come to Shermantown, because I'd discovered when trips home were sporadic, everyone wants a piece of you and there are hurt feelings for anyone you didn't make time for.

Dylan pulled out his phone and scrolled through photos. There was something boyish about how excited he was to show off his kids. I'd already seen the first one he showed me. "That's Malcolm, our little dare devil." In this one, they were in a proper photo studio. Malcolm was maybe a year old? I didn't have the best sense of age around kids that little. He belied the collared shirt-sweater-vest-khakis-loafers his parents had dressed him up in, crawling on the floor toward the camera, head cocked up with a smile that could only be described as mischievous. Dylan was fuzzy, leaning forward from a stool, reaching. Wendy, his wife was a little clearer. She sat back, head back, open-mouthed laughing in a way that seemed posed to me, but maybe the photographer caught her in just the right moment.

We went to high school with Wendy. I didn't really know her. She was two years younger than us.

Two years would've felt like a big deal then—a senior dating a sophomore, or a guy in community college dating a high school senior. Put it in the context of a marriage with school-aged kids. Put it in the context of a life and two years was nothing at all. Case in point, when I got charged with wrestling a girl, five, six years younger, older, it didn't matter at all. She was a worker of my generation who got in the business around the same time, watched the same wrestlers growing up, had likely as not traveled through the same territories, working under the same promoters, just in a different sequence. We knew the same people. Two years was no difference at all.

Kids were a difference. Doesn't matter how old. A change in identity. I'd known the Dylan whose dad watched wrestling, so he watched wrestling. Now, he was Dylan, first and foremost, dad to these kids who watched wrestling too. Dylan showed me the photos to corroborate, no telling if the focus on wrestling was for my benefit, or organic because his kids were as wrestle-crazed as the two of us once were.

"The funny thing is, I'd stopped watching. I mean, you and me finish high school and we're at the pinnacle—The Rock, Stone Cold. Then, what? John Cena. I'd still check out WrestleMania if I remembered it was happening or if someone was having a party, but that was it."

I remembered a party. Curt Wojtanowski—a fair-weather fan if there ever was one—hosted a get together for WrestleMania 17, the one where Stone Cold Steve Austin beat The Rock but had to turn heel to do it, beating his opponent over and over with a steel chair. Curt gave me a hard time because, unlike the other girls, I wasn't there just because my boyfriend liked wrestling. I liked wrestling, and he lorded it over me that girls don't really like wrestling, like he knew more about it than me because he'd watched in his tighty-whities when Hulk Hogan beat The Macho Man and now he was watching again when wrestling was back in style. I remembered chicken wings dripping in buffalo sauce and greasy pizza and that less than three months later I left Shermantown to become a wrestler.

"I kept tabs on you," Dylan said.

The waitress dropped off my black coffee, Dylan's Coke. She was thin, pimple-faced. Not far out of high school herself, I'd guess. She wrote our orders verbatim in her notepad, none of the bravado of more seasoned waitresses who assured customers they'd remember everything. I preferred the studious type, the record keepers. They never got the order wrong.

"I'd search your name on the Internet—try to keep track of all your gimmicks. And when YouTube came out, I got to see some of your matches."

He'd bought copies of the first VHS tapes and DVDs I had matches on. Low-res, low-quality stuff, where I was curtain jerking or working bathroom break matches in the middle of the card. The promoters got mad when YouTube became a thing—people putting up matches for free, the writing on the wall that tape revenue was going to be a thing of the past. I was happy about it, though. A lot of us were. Convinced ourselves that being on the Internet was as good as being on TV where anyone might find our matches, where we might be discovered.

"I remember the first time. You were wearing these purple pants and a gold top."

I remembered that era. That persona. I played a gypsy-type, long before anyone thought to call a term like that culturally insensitive. I did an approximation of a belly dance on my way to the ring, except I'd never learned to belly dance—I'm not sure I'd ever even seen one—so I did the best that my boyfriend at the time and I could come up with. I thought it was sort of sexy then, but when I've looked back at footage it proved even more embarrassing than I'd feared.

I'd get five minutes—if I was lucky with a veteran, but often as not with a girl as green as I was. Usually prettier than me. It didn't take long to settle into my role as a solid hand who could make girls who barely trained look a lot better than they were. I still rushed, though. Trying to get all my spots in—always something off the top rope—before the veterans got through about slowing down. About how less is more and how every wrestler has a bump card—a number of falls to the canvas they can take before their body gives out and they'll have to retire. No one knows how many bumps they have in them, but a bump off the top rope sure as hell counted for three or four holes punched from the card.

"I couldn't believe it, watching you. I know we messed around in the tennis court and you were a daredevil. But here you are, really *doing it*—dropkicks and hurricanranas and moonsaults." He shook his head in wonder. "And then on TV I see Randy Orton chinlocking somebody to sleep—not just the wrestler, but the audience too. It's such a snoozefest. They call those rest holds right? So both guys can catch their breath?"

The waitress was back she left my egg-white omelette, his Belgian waffle covered in powdered sugar, surrounded by a ring of whipped cream and halved strawberries, a square of butter melting on top. He slathered it all in maple syrup.

The idea of rest holds got out on the Internet—that a chinlock, a bearhug, a full nelson were designed to let the wrestlers both relax for a minute and gather their strength for another flurry of action. It's not untrue, but there are other reasons, like letting the crowd settle so they'll pop for the next big move. "There's a difference between TV wrestling and what you see in the arena." I cut into my omelette. There was too much cheese on it, so I scraped some to the side. "If you're on TV, there are broadcasters and a lot of fans don't realize they're telling half the story—telling you how to feel. The TV wrestlers grab a hold and they're giving the color commentator the chance to the tell story behind the match, about how this body part has been injured for years or about what a technician one guy is or why this hold is so dangerous it's been banned in sixteen states."

I laughed at myself a little at that last part, because it was absurd, but I did know a commentator once, coming down from the big leagues to record the vocal track over our big show the promoter was going to sell on DVD, and he made a big deal out of holds that were banned or illegal in amateur wrestling because of the risk of causing so much pain they could cause a psychological break. It was all make-believe. One of the nights he showed up drunk and wound up laughing at himself. The promoter canned him and scrapped the whole DVD project because it would cost too much to rerecord the commentary. A lot of the boys in the locker room were mad because they were counting on the DVD royalties and it took everything I had in me not to laugh at them. Hang around this business long enough, and you know there aren't any DVD royalties coming your way—even if the DVD does come to fruition and does sell enough copies to make up production costs (not to mention how improbable those propositions were). Promoters were charlatans and grifters. The best you could count on was the money they promised you the night you wrestled, and even then *the gate wasn't quite what we expected* or *the arena hit me with a fee to use their lighting guy, so I'm a little light.* Always, *I'll make it up to you at the next town.*

Dylan was starry-eyed, a little whipped cream on his lower lip. He had crow's feet at the corners of his eyes and some gray in his hair, but in a moment like this I could see the teenager in him again.

I wanted to tell him I've been in a thousand diners like this, a thousand late nights. I watched Bruiser Magee eat a dozen eggs, twenty strips of bacon and chase it all down with two pots of coffee. I was there when Lelah Dorengo and seven-foot-tall Potter Hoytes disappeared to the ladies' room together and locked themselves inside and the whole diner could hear what they were up to minutes before a waitress, then the manager caught on, beating on the door. Lelah and Potter didn't rush themselves, but when they were done, Potter opened the door and came out casually, stood chest to face with the manager and dared him to say something more about how he was going to call the police; the manager said nothing. I was there when Johnny Flex got into it with Wheelbarrow Willy because he thought he'd slept with his girl and there was the night Sissy Folgers called me out to the parking lot because she was high and thought I'd been too stiff with her in the ring that night. I stepped outside and body slammed her into the windshield of a Corolla. Next thing I knew, someone was throwing me in the backseat of a car and peeling out before the police arrived, car alarm wailing into the night.

All these diners, all these nights, all these stories I could tell. But I never experienced what Dylan did a couple minutes later, midway through showing me a photo of Malcolm holding his little sister Missy, when a text notification showed up. First name only. Wendy.

He turned the phone away to read the full message, then text something back. He was still typing when he started talking to me again. "I love my kids. I love my wife. I love my life." He paused, tapping a couple times more on the screen before the phone made a *whoosh* sound of a text going out. "But I don't think I'll ever get rid of that part of me that regrets not hitting the road with you. I could've been a wrestler too. Can you imagine that? Had that whole life?"

I heard the regrets of a life not lived. I'd heard it before from a hundred fans who hung around for autographs after shows. And there was the obvious corollary, as he turned back to showing me pictures of Malcolm grown up and his daughter Missy and of the professional photos they had done at an orchard last autumn that maybe I, too, missed out on something when I chose wrestling, moving territory to territory. Didn't I wish I'd stayed home and built a life like his?

Every opportunity chosen is the choice to regret another thing. Dylan's phone vibrated in his hand. Another text from Wendy.

She called him home, of course. Asked how much later he'd be out. Reminded him the kids had school in the morning and he had work and she missed him and hoped she'd get to see him before she went to sleep and she hoped he didn't get too carried away having late-night breakfast with his high school sweetheart and making the kind of choices he would have in high school and he'd regret by the light of day. Something like that.

Dylan looked sheepish. Like a younger version of himself I'd once known whose mom told him he had to visit his grandmother on Sunday when he and I had plans to go to the mall. "It looks like I'm going to turn into a pumpkin." He tipped back his Coke, foregoing the straw, drinking down the dregs, sliding a half-melted ice chip into his mouth. "It was good to see you."

"You too."

We haggled over who'd pick up the bill (I paid, he tipped). I got up first. We walked out together. He held the door for me. We hugged outside. We'd parked our cars on opposite ends of the lot.

The speakers spat static after I'd turned on my Civic. I'd forgotten that I lost signal more and more as I'd traveled north on the turnpike. I'd turned the dial for a while but got preoccupied as I drew closer to my destination. I turned down the volume there in the parking lot before I put the car into reverse to pull out, then put it in drive to pull away.

Lights flashed. Dylan offering one last goodbye as I drove past. I didn't bother to stop or even look. We'd said enough goodbyes already.

It took a beat longer to realize I hadn't turned my headlights on. It might not have been Dylan, but anyone at all pointing out that I was driving out into the dark and no one could see me coming.

I turned my lights on.

Dylan was heading home.

I was heading onward.

SHELAGH POWERS JOHNSON

Wreckage

That the truth of it all could be reduced to a tidy square of text seemed impossible: her undoing nestled between other slender catastrophes, tabloid trash in the express line at the supermarket razing her life in ten words.

Theo was tucked into the front of the cart, sucking pear purée from a pouch they hadn't yet paid for; Alice was a sleeping bundle on her hip. She felt a reflexive urge to hand them over to someone in that moment—a police officer, a woman with children, the types of people they'd been instructed to look for in a crowd if they ever got lost.

Theo's dangling legs kicked at her stomach as she steered the cart out of line and toward the exit, a silent protest against this break from their routine, this pull in the thread of his ironed little life. She lifted him out and balanced him on her other hip as she headed for the parking lot, groceries abandoned, the baby food pouch clenched in his dimpled fist now a tiny first crime.

When they got home, she deposited a sleeping Alice into her toddler bed, lifting one socked foot to her lips for the last time. She left Theo in the kitchen with the housekeeper and said goodbye to him with a kiss on the head and the salve of a lie: *see you tomorrow, my guy.* But he wasn't hers, and tomorrow she would no longer exist within the taut radius of his three-year-old universe.

She left before anyone could tell her to leave, exiling herself before the world did it for her. She slipped an envelope of cash under her landlord's door to sever her month-to-month lease, left her supplies behind in Ben's studio like an offering, a meager atonement: slabs of cool, shapeless clay stacked high on the shelves, a mason jar packed tight with knives, the blank face of her sculpting wheel. The rumors had begun churning their way through social media, gathering dirt and grime along the way, and they'd surely landed in Ben's open hands by now. She imagined the facts of what she'd done flashing across his screen, coming to him in pieces, shrapnel slicing at him until eventually they hit bone. She couldn't bear the idea of seeing the naked hurt on his face, of hearing it in his voice over the phone, and so she'd sent him one line of text while sitting in traffic and then blocked his number. *I told you I'd fuck it all up.*

*

The rental was a few hours outside the city, shabby and uninviting, a husk of a place that might once have been charming. But that was what she wanted: to be somewhere no one would ever choose to be, where open days stretched blindly into weeks until she was forgotten. The house was available for as long as she needed it—a fact advertised like a gift but with the mildewed stench of desperation.

There was a narrow creek out back, and on her first afternoon she walked along the rocky seam where the dirt turned to mud, the water cold and rushing after a season of rain. The rocks were slimy with moss, slick and loose beneath her bare feet; she liked the feel of the ground shifting under her, a whole network invisibly arranging and rearranging itself. She dipped her fingertips into the water to feel the silky earth beneath her hands, and the mud was wet clay in her palms: amorphous, ready to be anything. She let it slide between her fingers and back into the cool water. What she needed was not yielding tenderness; what she needed was a hard fist of earth, something that would fight her back, that wouldn't grow soft and pliable in the warm cradle of her skin—she needed a writhing fever to churn her sickness to the surface.

She thought of Ben's studio back in the city—the vases she'd sculpted to line the sills of the windows, the animal figurines and piles of seashells and lone body parts that she'd carved from clay and then painted to look slick and organic: a bright red lump of heart, white stretches of bone, the alien coil of intestines. She wondered how long it would be before he threw them away, or if perhaps they were already gone. She wondered for a moment if maybe he'd broken them all, slammed them against the floor and walls, crunched the shattered pieces beneath his feet. But he wasn't that sort of person, more likely to wrap them carefully in newspaper and send them to one of her friends than allow himself the luxury of destruction.

*

She pushed her thumbs deep into the wet heft of clay, the sun hot on her bare back. Her phone had been buzzing relentlessly with unfamiliar numbers, and she watched the notifications pile up on the screen: two, three, four new voicemails, text messages in the double digits. She knew some of the messages had to be from Ben, and her cheeks flushed with shame at the idea of him realizing he'd been blocked, borrowing other people's phones to contact her. She stared at the red circle above the message icon, a blemish begging to be picked at, raw with the promise of pain and relief. But she couldn't stand the thought of hearing what he had to say, of absorbing his hurt without giving in to her own, and so she swiped the notifications away and returned to her work. She'd begun to use mud from the creek—left to bake in the sun, it hardened to a dusty pink and held its form—though most of what she made she tossed, a collection of unfinished creatures collecting in the yard like bones.

She often thought about the children while she worked, remembered their chubby hands plunging into tubs of play-doh, pinching the neon clay into approximations of living things. She pictured the orange-brown freckles dusted across Theo's nose, the bright honey of Alice's eyes, her pupils like perfect fossils encased in resin. She could still hear the sound of their little voices, all husky breath and grand pronouncements, profound and matter-of-fact in the way only children can be. She knew she didn't deserve to grieve any of it—not the children, not Ben or her job or her life—and the sickening guilt of what she'd done felt selfish, indulgent. There was nowhere to put the pain that came with hurting people; all she could do was swallow it down and let the shards carve away at her from the inside.

She dipped her hands into the bowl of water at her side, then wrapped them around the slimy curve of clay that sat in front of her. She'd begun chiseling the delicate features of a woman into it, trimming away at the clay as if she were unearthing ancient bones, searching for a face buried beneath its surface. But she couldn't get the eyes right: they stared up at her like marbles, eerie and wrong, unblinking in their judgment. She grabbed her sculpting knife and began sawing at the top section of the woman's head, slicing along the bridge of her nose and cutting clean through. Then she removed the severed clay and smashed it between her fists, feeling immediately relieved, as if she'd averted a crisis, avoided shaping something malevolent into existence. She often thought about her art this way, secretly wondering if she could infuse good into the atmosphere by creating enough beauty, or if sculpting something grotesque meant living in a world that was just the slightest bit uglier, darker.

She pressed her knuckles into the bottom half of the woman's head, considered whether to hollow her out into a bowl, into a flower pot, into some other pleasing shape, some benign and practical vessel. She fussed with the woman's edges for a few minutes. She pressed shallow wrinkles into the bow of her lips to show that she'd lived a real life, smoothed out the contours of her cheekbones to suggest that the woman had once been beautiful. But she knew she was trying to push life into something lifeless, knead her palms against a heart that couldn't beat. She knew that when she was done this halved and emptied version of the woman would be discarded, another casualty added to the wreckage.

*

The tabloids had called it an affair, but the word had an unearned heft to it, a suggestion of intimacy that wasn't there; she didn't even have Andrew's number saved in her phone. The articles had left little to the imagination, published in the sorts of magazines that print first and asks questions later. Some of the details had been sleazy embellishments—there had been no private jet trysts, no salacious photos sent back and forth; she hadn't traded sex and discretion for the promise of future movie roles or gallery shows—but the seeds of the story, the parts from which the untruths grew, were all that really mattered.

The formless thing between them had in fact been ordinary and predictable, so clichéd that its doomed trajectory may as well have been mapped from the start. Andrew's pursuit of her had seemed both impossible and inevitable, the push of a bud from the tight bead of a leaf, the slow revolution of a plant toward the sun. Their mistakes splayed out in front of her the moment his fingers grazed the small of her back and lingered there like a question, and for half a year after that her life had been cleanly bisected. She'd spent her days playing pretend with his children, doling out snacks, giving baths and telling stories and singing lullabies. She'd aired silly grievances with the housekeeper and made polite chitchat with the children's mother. After work each day she'd gone to the studio to sculpt while Ben painted, ordered takeout and watched old episodes of *Curb Your Enthusiasm* curled into the warm hollow of his open arms. Her everyday life was quiet, subdued—contentment washed over her like the predictable comfort of their nightly reruns.

But then there were spaces of time layered between these things, hidden and malignant: afternoons spread out across a king-sized bed during naptime, or pressed into the tight air of the pantry as cartoons chattered in the other room, doing her job for her. Andrew became a habit she couldn't shake, like biting her nails to the quick even though it stung, even though the slender pleasure of whittling away at herself only left her feeling sore and ashamed.

She had no excuses for what she'd done, and she didn't bother blaming Andrew for any of it; disdain for his part in things seemed as pointless as hating a door that slams on your finger or a cement wall that dings your car. She'd made the same mistake over and over, piled her regrets like the bones of her half-formed creatures, hidden and discarded. She'd allowed her mind to slacken around the thought of all the suffering she might cause, all the lives she'd likely dismantle, until her guilt was shapeless, viscous. Then she'd say the things she knew she ought to say whenever she and Andrew were alone, when she'd hear the telling click of the door closing behind him: *wait, stop, this is wrong, we shouldn't, we shouldn't, we shouldn't.* And then she'd do it anyway, a silent resignation to something she wasn't sure she even wanted, like a dessert she ate simply because it was there. Because she kept mistaking emptiness for hunger.

TONY MARTELLO

By Land Or Sea?

The couple lands at the Kona International Airport. Taylor has a plan to propose to his girlfriend of eight months. He knows he must take her to the hottest place on earth where neither lover has been before. This one is not like his first wife who hounded him daily for leaving shoes in the entryway and pressured him to climb the corporate ladder to no avail.

As they exit the stairs from Aloha Airlines, Taylor dreams, "This one is more like *Pele* whose veins warm the earth to her core, whose arms embrace me with molten magma, and whose fingers steam at the touch of the Pacific waters!" They proceed to the baggage claim and retrieve their suitcases. Taylor leads them to a long line for a rental car. He walks over to the marketing pamphlets stacked up against the wall where visitors search for tourist attractions and endless activities. He grabs a thick pamphlet and takes it to his girlfriend, "Lana, since we're going to be here for a few days, try and find a few activities for us. I'm going to check on getting a Cherokee" While Lana browses the tracts, Taylor walks around the corner where he can't be overheard. He approaches a local guy behind the desk of the jeep rental line, "Hey, I have a question for you. I want to take my lady to the place where the lava flows to the ocean. "The local guy replies, "Ah, you mean Kilauea, where da lava flows in the ocean by Kalapana, or into Kapoho Bay?" Taylor's eyes widen, "yeah, I think that's the spot. The desk clerk continues, "Da way I see it, brah, is you can go by land, or you can go by sea." Taylor's right eye squints upward, "I see, what is the hike like to get there by foot?" "Ho, brah, it's like a long two-mile hike and you get da *vog*... you know, da kine volcanic fog, it can get thick, and sting your eyes."

The local clerk warns, "Your lady not gone like da vog, braddah, you might try to go by boat and go down to Kalapana, and into Kapoho Bay, it's unreal, you gone blow her mind!" Taylor likes this idea and asks the clerk more questions, "Where do I go to sign up?" The local replies, "Try Lava Boat Trips," They have an aluminum boat and can take out like ten people per journey. It's unreal."

What would you do? Weave through dangerous billows of volcanic fog or brave the molten sea in an aluminum boat with boiling water surrounding you?

Taylor envisioned them walking across super-hot lava rocks while the soles of their shoes melt, sticking to the rugged terrain. Lana may like the tactile touch of the young hot earth but what about the catatonic smell of sulfuric acid sizzling all around her? On the other hand, she may appreciate a romantic boat ride along the wild and unpredictable Kalapana coastline. Whichever way he chose would have its drawbacks. The boat ride seemed scarier with the potential of getting lost at sea or capsizing, but the smoky hike seemed harsh and uncomfortable. If anyone could handle hiking in the *vog*, it was Lana, as she had been in many fires in both houses and dry land. She had been working as a firefighter for fifteen years in which five of those were fighting wildland California state fires. She was obsessed with fire-its bright color, mystery, and power. Because of her experience managing fire and its destructive effects, Taylor had to top it-he had to present her with the ultimate fire experience. Taylor knew that he must be comfortable if he was going to ask this woman to marry him, so he chose the boat trip and called to schedule a Lava Boat tour for day number two of their getaway. He returned to his fiancé standing in line. "Lana, pick an activity tomorrow because I have plans for us on Thursday." Her curiosity peaked, "Sounds mysterious. I've been reading about the Humuhumu triggerfish that can swim through hot water and warm vents. Have you heard of that one?" Taylor laughs, "Humu-humu-unuku-unuku-apuaa. It's the Hawaii state fish."

Lana chuckles, "I read an interesting legend about how this fish represented a Hawaiian leader who was piglike, had a snout and was sneaky in his shape-shifting ways. One day he met Pele in all her fiery boldness. She had steam billowing off her hair and the water around her was boiling to the touch. He fell in love with her and asked her to marry him. Soon thereafter, she realized he was too piglike and snidely, so she condemned him to the underworld where he turned into a colorful triggerfish that roams the islands today." At this moment Taylor knew he made the right decision to propose via boat ride. Now, he must figure out how to deliver the proposal and put the ring on her finger.

How would you do it?

That morning they wake up early and brew some Kona coffee. They scoop up some papaya with granola and yogurt and a squirt of lemon and enjoyed a nice breakfast. On the way to Pahoa, they stop and swim in the volcanic pools nestled in the lava rocks. They arrive at the park where the boat ride begins. The captain is hosing down his boat and checking all the parts to make sure it is in full working condition. Lana tells Taylor, "I'm going to use the bathroom." She walks over to the restrooms.

Taylor seizes an opportunity to ask the captain about an idea he has. "Hey captain, we are scheduled to go on a boat ride with you at 7:00 pm, I am wondering how I can surprise my girlfriend with a marriage proposal on the ride?" The salt-crusted man in his late forties drops the hose and smiles...I got one for you brah that will blow her mind. I have always wanted someone to be brave enough to try it but have had no takers."

Taylor steps closer blazing with curiosity, "Tell me more!" The captain chuckles a bit and says, ok, I must reveal one of our surprises that you may like for your proposal..., you promise not to tell anyone aboard the ship? Taylor obliges, "for sure, captain." The captain continues, "we dip a bucket into the 120-degree ocean water and pull it up for our tourists to feel once we get to the lava pouring in the ocean." Taylor leans in closer, and the captain suggests, "I will drop the ring in the bucket after I pull it from the ocean, but you must encourage your girlfriend to be the volunteer to test the waters if you will?" Taylor agrees, "she will for sure. She is brave and adventuresome. Oh, no, here she comes." Taylor hands the captain the ring, the captain nods agreeing to a plan that will seal Taylor's fate in marriage.

The boat launches at 7:00 under a starry night sky. The tour motors up and down over the vast ocean next to the largest mountains in the world if you measure it from the seafloor to the top of the island. Taylor and Lana gaze at the sky and sea when they notice a large ember-like vein slithering into the ocean. Steam sizzles above the glowing orange vein flowing from the landmass of Hawaii. As the boat approaches the lava flowing into the ocean the captain announces, "We are going to drift here for a while, who would like to test the waters for us and do a temperature check?" The captain slyly reaches into his pocket while the deckhand is dropping the bucket into the water when suddenly Taylor spots the ring flying across the boat deck and hears a small thud. He jumps to pick it up and raises his hand to volunteer all in one fell swoop. "Wow, it feels like a hot jacuzzi, wait, what is this? I feel a rock in here!" Taylor lifts the ring out of the water and holds it up, "Lana, will you marry me?" The crew cheers and Lana says, "yes" but Taylor can't hear her under the roar of the crowd!

CONTRIBUTORS

Angel T. Dionne is an associate professor of English literature at the University of Moncton Edmundston campus. She holds a PhD in creative writing from the University of Pretoria and is the founding editor of *Vroom Lit Magazine*. Her writing and art have been featured in several experimental publications. She is the author of two chapbooks: *Inanimate Objects* (Bottlecap Press, 2022) and *Mormyridae* (LJMcD Communications, 2024). She is also the author of a collection of short fiction, *Sardines* (Clarion Lit, 2023). Dionne is the co-editor of *Rape Culture 101: Programming Change* (Demeter Press, 2020). The included poems are from her debut full-length poetry collection *Bird Ornaments* (Broken Tribe, 2025).

Ann Calandro is a writer, mixed media collage artist, and classical piano student. For many years she worked as a copyeditor. Her fiction, creative nonfiction, and poetry have been published in literary journals and anthologies. Her artwork has appeared in juried exhibits and literary journals. She wrote and illustrated three children's books published by Shanti Arts Press. Calandro was born and raised in New York City.

Chad Weeden's work has appeared in *The Midwest Quarterly, Pedestal Magazine, Jabberwock Review, The Asheville Poetry Review*, and elsewhere. He is a portrait photographer and lives in Rhode Island. For more information, please visit chadweedenphoto.com. His debut poetry collection titled *the ice stayed but the water left* is forthcoming by Broken Tribe Press in 2025.

David Holper is the author of the 2025 collection *Bord för En*. He has published three earlier collections of poetry *Language Lessons: A Linguistic Hejira* (Deeper Magic Press), *The Bridge* (Sequoia Song Publications), *64 Questions* (March Street Press), as well as one novel, *The Church of the Very Last Chance* (Deeper Magic Press). His poems and stories have appeared in numerous journals and anthologies. He lives in Eureka, California, where he served as the City of Eureka's inaugural poet laureate from August 2019-August 2021. He loves that Eureka is far enough away from the madness of civilization that he can still hear the Canada geese calling. His website is www.davidholper.com

Eleanor Keisman is an American writer, born in New York. After dropping out of high school, she worked her way up through community colleges in Honolulu, Denver, and upstate New York, finally transferring to Stony Brook University on Long Island, where she studied Fine Arts, but ultimately earned her BA in Liberal Arts from The New School in Manhattan. She left the US and spent over a decade living, studying, and working in France, Czechia, Poland, China, and Austria. Her academic career continued at the University of Vienna, where she studied German and English linguistics. She then worked for a legal tech startup as a bilingual copywriter and marketing consultant (earning an MBA in the process) and an educational NGO, organizing international exchange internships. She holds an MFA in creative writing from Drexel University. She co-organizes an English-language writing group in Vienna, Austria, where she lives. *New Animal* is her first novella.

Jianqing Zheng is the author of *Visual Chords*, *The Dog Years of Reeducation*, *A Way of Looking*, and five poetry chapbooks. He is the editor of several scholarly books, including *Conversations with Dana Gioia* and *Sonia Sanchez's Poetic Spirit through Haiku*; and coeditor of four scholarly books, including *Dana Gioia: Poet & Critic*. He is a professor of English at Mississippi Valley State University, where he founded and edits the *Journal of Ethnic American Literature* and *Valley Voices: A Literary Review*. His poems have appeared in numerous magazines, including *Another Chicago Magazine*, *Arkansas Review*, *Birmingham Poetry Review*, *Cimarron Review*, *Hanging Loose*, *Mississippi Review*, and *Spillway*.

J. Dominic Patacsil is a fiction writer based in Washington, D.C. He was awarded the 2023 *Los Angeles Review* Flash Fiction Prize, and his stories have appeared in *New Ohio Review, Third Coast Magazine,* and *Raleigh Review*, among others. He is a graduate of the MFA program at the University of New Hampshire. *Bald Spot* is his debut collection of stories.

John Oliver Hodges was born in Tallahassee. A collection of short fiction and photography *Luv Slaps* was released by Broken Tribe Press in 2025. His other published books include *Quizzleboon* (a novel), *The Love Box* (short stories) and *Eating My Name* (a memoir on Kindle). As a teenager he was guitarist for the American hardcore band, Hated Youth.

J.R. Solonche's most recent book is *Barren Road* (Serving House, 2025). Nominated for the National Book Award, the Eric Hoffer Book Award, and nominated three times for the Pulitzer Prize, Solonche is the author of 40 books of poetry and coauthor of another. He lives in the Hudson Valley.

Kenneth Pobo is the author of twenty-one chapbooks and ten full-length collections. *It Gets Dark So Soon Now* is his most recent collection (Broken Tribe, 2025). Recent books include *Bend of Quiet* (Blue Light Press) and *Loplop in a Red City* (Circling Rivers). His work has appeared in *Asheville Poetry Review, North Dakota Quarterly, Amsterdam Quarterly, Nimrod, Mudfish, Hawaii Review,* and elsewhere.

Logan Garner is a Hoosier/PNW poet residing on Oregon's north coast. Winner of the Neahkahnie Mountain Poetry Prize, his work has been featured in *Orca Literary Journal, The Elevation Review, The Salal Review, Flying Island* and others, as well as Tupelo Press's 30/30 project in 2024. He is the author of collections *Here, in the Floodplain* (Plan B Press, 2023) and *The Sin of Feeding Wild Birds* (forthcoming, Broken Tribe Press, 2025).

Matt Thomas is a smallholder farmer, engineer, and poet. *Cicada, Dog & Song* is his second full-length collection. His first, *Disappearing by the Math*, was published in 2024 by Silver Bow. A chapbook, *Foxy Love: All-American Poems* will be published by Kelsay Books in 2026. His poetry has appeared in *Triggerfish Critical Review, Ponder Review, Hampden-Sydney Review, Hiram Review, Dunes Review, Avalon Literary Review, Galway Review, Milk House Review, Cleaver Magazine, River Heron Review, The Thieving Magpie, Common House Magazine, Slab Magazine,* and elsewhere. www.mattthomaspoetry.com

Matthew McConkey is the author of three novels: *Home Again, Maple Lane*, and *Summerland*. He is also the author of two short story collections, *Everything Fades in Time* and *Scarecrows and Shadows,* the latter of which contains "Estate Sale." He lives in Tennessee.

Max Talley is the author of the 2025 collection *Destroy Me Gently, Please* (Serving House). He has two previous story collections, *My Secret Place* (Main Street Rag) and *When The Night Breathes Electric*. He is also the author of three published novels. His writing has appeared in numerous journals and he's been nominated for four Pushcart Prizes. He lives somewhere along I-40, on the long, lonely road between New Mexico and Southern California. www.maxtalley.com

Michael Chin was born and raised in Utica, New York and currently lives in Las Vegas with his wife and son, where he teaches for the UNLV Honors College. He's the author of seven full-length books, including his novel, *My Grandfather's an Immigrant, and So is Yours* (Cowboy Jamboree Press, 2021). Chin won the 2017-2018 Jean Leiby Chapbook Award from *The Florida Review* as well as *Bayou Magazine's* 2014 James Knudsen Prize for Fiction. He is the author of *Territories* (Serving House Books, 2025). miketchin.com

Mildred Kiconco Barya, a North Carolina-based writer and poet of East African descent, teaches and lectures globally. She is the author of four poetry books, including *The Animals of My Earth School* (Terrapin Books), which received the 2025 Jacobs/Jones African American Literary Prize. Her work has been published in the *New England Review, The Cincinnati Review, Shenandoah, Tin House, The Forge*, and elsewhere. *Hands in Clay* is her fifth full-length poetry collection. mildredbarya.com

Narya Deckard is an Appalachian writer who lives in Valdese, NC. She holds degrees from UNC Asheville and Lenoir-Rhyne University. She's had poems curated in journals such as *Tiny Seed Press, The Dead Mule School, Eternal Haunted Summer, and Kakalak Anthology*. She teaches writing at Lenoir-Rhyne University. Her debut poetry collection titled *Wolfcraft* won the Tribe MFA Award and is forthcoming by Broken Tribe Press in 2025.

Rebecca A. Durham is a poet, botanist, and visual artist. She is the author of the award-winning ecopoetry books *Be Still Mere Molecule, Half-life of Empathy,* and *Loss/Less*. Durham holds an undergraduate degree in Biology, master's degrees in Botany and Creative Writing, and an Interdisciplinary PhD. She has worked across the west as a botanist and ecologist, with over twenty years in western Montana where she lives with her daughter. Find more of her work at rebeccadurham.net

Ricardo Moran is a past recipient of the Peter K. Hixson Memorial Award for Poetry. His writing has been published in *Beatific Magazine, Midwest Quarterly, Perceptions Magazine, East Jasmine Review, The Seattle Star*, and *Willa Cather Review*. He currently lives in Albania; enjoys traveling; and learning how to say "good morning" in as many languages as possible. In every timeline, you can find him reading, writing, and plotting right here: www.ricardomoranwriter.com

Rick Mulkey is the author of six collections, including *All These Hungers, Ravenous: New & Selected Poems, Toward Any Darkness, Before the Age of Reason,* and *Bluefield Breakdown.* His awards include the Hawthornden Fellowship, the Charles Angoff Award from *The Literary Review,* and the Gearhart Poetry Prize from *Southeast Review.*

Rita Signorelli-Pappas is the author of three poetry collections *The Chameleon* (2025), *Labyrinth* (2019), and *Satyr's Wife* (2010) all published by Serving House Books. Her poems have been published in *Poetry, Shenandoah, Southwest Review, Prairie Schooner, The Literary Review, Poet Lore, The Women's Review of Books, Southern Poetry Review, Notre Dame Review,* and other publications. Rita is a regular poetry reviewer for *World Literature Today,* and her fiction has appeared in *Helicon Nine, Italian Americana, Helicon Nine, Farmer's Market, Crosscurrents,* and *VIA.*

Shelagh Powers Johnson received her MFA in Fiction from American University and is currently working on her PhD in English. She teaches Literature and Creative Writing at Bowie State University, where she also serves as faculty editor of the university's literary magazine, *The Torch.* Her work has appeared in *The Portland Review, Ghost Parachute, The Plentitudes,* and *The Grace and Gravity Anthologies,* among others, and her writing has been nominated for Best Microfiction and Best Small Fictions. Her debut collection *A History of Existing Life* was published by Broken Tribe in 2025. You can find her at www.shelaghjohnson.com.

Tony Martello is a family therapist by day and a masterful weaver of short fiction by night. He's the creative force behind *Flat Spell Tales, Under the Curtain,* and *Of Song & Stitches,* with all three brought vividly to life on Audible. His evocative stories have found homes in renowned publications like *October Hill Magazine, New English Review, Atherton Review,* and *Short Edition.* When he's not crafting compelling narratives, Tony enjoys life in scenic San Luis Obispo, CA with his wife and daughters.

WK Lawrence is the author of twelve books including two novels *Highway Zero* (2023) and *The Punk and the Professor* (2017). Selections included are from *Four for Four, which is his fourth collection of poems*. He is originally from New York.

www.ingramcontent.com/pod-product-compliance
Lightning Source LLC
Chambersburg PA
CBHW020047310726
48970CB00007B/2455